MODERN BAND METHO

Bass

Book 1

Scott Burstein
Spencer Hale
Mary Claxton
Dave Wish

Contributors:
Tony Sauza, Clayton McIntyre, Lauren Brown, Joe Panganiban

To access audio and video visit:
www.halleonard.com/mylibrary

Enter Code
1543-4441-9645-7444

ISBN 978-1-5400-7669-4

Visit Hal Leonard Online at
www.halleonard.com

Contact us:
Hal Leonard
7777 West Bluemound Road
Milwaukee, WI 53213
Email: info@halleonard.com

In Europe, contact:
Hal Leonard Europe Limited
42 Wigmore Street
Marylebone, London, W1U 2RN
Email: info@halleonardeurope.com

In Australia, contact:
Hal Leonard Australia Pty. Ltd.
4 Lentara Court
Cheltenham, Victoria, 3192 Australia
Email: info@halleonard.com.au

Introduction **4**
Parts of the Bass Guitar; Tuning; Basic Technique; Notation

Section 1 .... **7**
The Notes E, G, and C; Two-Note Groove; The Song Chart; Composing with Three Chords/Notes
Full Band Repertoire: *Can't Stop the Feeling, Without You, Send My Love, Wake Me Up, I Gotta Feeling*

Section 2 .... **12**
The Note A; Reading Bass Tab; Finger Exercises; Muting Strings; Four-Note Groove; Whole and Half Notes
Full Band Repertoire: *Low Rider, Heathens*

Section 3 .... **16**
The Note D; Chromatic Riffs; Quarter and Eighth Notes; Creating a Groove; Composing a Bass Line
Full Band Repertoire: *Dazed and Confused, Imagine, Best Day of My Life*

Section 4 .... **19**
Muting Notes; Writing Lyrics
Full Band Repertoire: *We Will Rock You, Back in Black, What Makes You Beautiful, Stir It Up*

Section 5 .... **22**
Muted Note Review; Notes, Chords, and Scales; Drum and Bass; Mastering the Grid

Section 6 .... **27**
Changing the Rhythm; The Music Staff
Full Band Repertoire: *Land of a Thousand Dances, Someone Like You*

Section 7 .... **32**
Rhythmic Patterns; Composing an Introduction
Full Band Repertoire: *Oye Como Va*

Section 8 .... **34**
Steady Eighth Notes; Syncopated Patterns; Reggae Bass Patterns
Full Band Repertoire: *Waka Waka*

Section 9 .... **39**
Note Length; Composing a Verse and Chorus; Major Pentatonic Scale
Full Band Repertoire: *Hey There Delilah, Haiti, Wild Thing, The Edge of Glory, Halo, Waiting in Vain, Best Day of My Life*

Section 10 .... **45**
Slides; Passing Tones; Applying Slides
Full Band Repertoire: *Kick, Push*

Section 11 .... **50**
Blues Scale; Chords as Riffs; Composing with Power Chords
Full Band Repertoire: *Umbrella*

Section 12 .... **55**
Full Band Repertoire: *Zombie*

Introduction

Welcome!

If you are reading this, you have already made the decision to learn to play bass so you can play some of your favorite songs. One of the best things about playing in a Modern Band is that you don't need much time to start jammin', but there are plenty of skills to learn and master over time too. Most popular musicians are able to perform in a wide variety of musical styles by playing grooves with different rhythms to accompany a vocalist. They often add memorable riffs, or short melodic phrases, that stay in your head all day. This method book is designed to teach you skills to play bass and create music in a variety of popular music styles—pop, rock, R&B, funk, hip-hop, and more. Let's get started!

Jam Tracks and Video Lessons

Use the audio Jam Tracks throughout this book to practice the songs and exercises. Also be sure to watch the included video lessons that demonstrate many of the techniques and concepts. To access all of the audio and video files for download or streaming, just visit *www.halleonard.com/mylibrary* and enter the code found on page 1 of this book.

Parts of the Bass Guitar

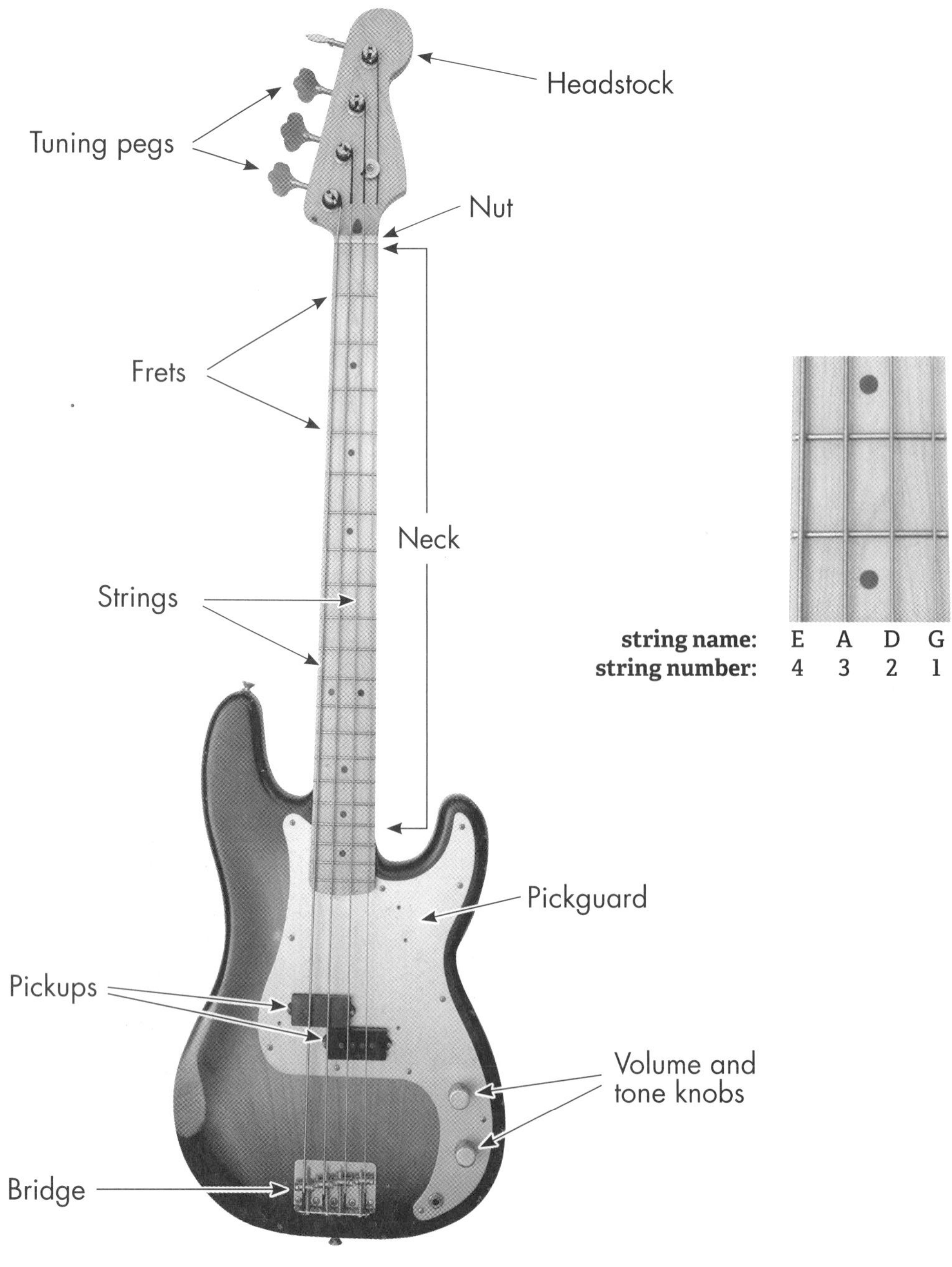

Tuning

Even if you're using perfect technique, your bass won't sound right if it's not in tune. Be sure to watch the video and tune your bass before you start playing.

Basic Technique

If you're playing a right-handed bass, hold the neck of the bass in your left hand and rest the body of the bass on your lap. If you're standing, you should use a strap to hold the instrument and adjust it to a comfortable height. If you're using a left-handed instrument, use the opposite hands.

The two most common ways to play the bass are fingerstyle and picking. Which technique you use is entirely up to you. Some players use different techniques for different styles of music.

With fingerstyle, you do not use a pick. Instead, place your right-hand thumb on the bass' pickup and alternate using your index and middle finger to play the strings, like two legs walking. Your fingers should fall into the thumb (when playing the low E string) or the next lower string (when playing any other string). When using a pick, place the pick between your thumb and index finger and pluck the string with the pick. Throughout this book, the term "picking" will refer to either technique.

Notation

The following bass graphics will be used throughout the book. The first is the **note diagram**. An open circle above the diagram tells you to play a string **open**, or without holding down any frets. If you see an "X" over a string, it means to not play that string. In this example, the note diagram tells you to play the 4th string open.

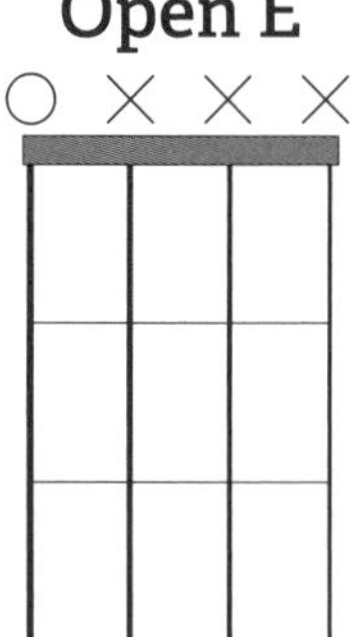

Another version of this graphic includes dots on the neck of the instrument. This shows you where to press down your finger on the neck of the instrument. In this example, the note diagram tells you to play the 3rd string while pressing down at the 3rd fret.

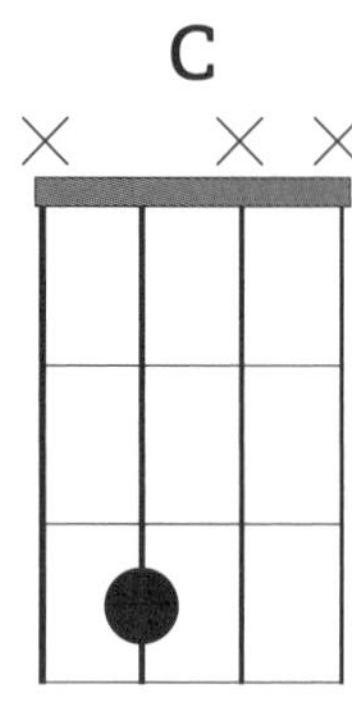

Next, let's look at how we notate rhythms. This is read left to right. Count these numbers steadily, "1, 2, 3, 4, 1, 2, 3, 4...," and play a note on the black numbers.

| 1 2 3 4 |

| 1 2 3 4 |

Learning rhythms and notes will improve your ability to "comp." **Comping** means using your musical knowledge to make up rhythms over a chord progression that fit a song's style.

This book is designed for you to learn alongside other Modern Band musicians so you can jam with your friends and classmates, but it can also be used as a stand-alone book to learn to play bass. Though some of the skills that you will be working on during each section will be different from those of the other instruments, all of the Full Band Songs are designed to be played by a whole band together. Now, let's start playing some music!

SECTION 1

Playing Bass Lines: One-Note Jam 

Play the open E string using the rhythms below. Feel free to create your own rhythms based on how the music moves you.

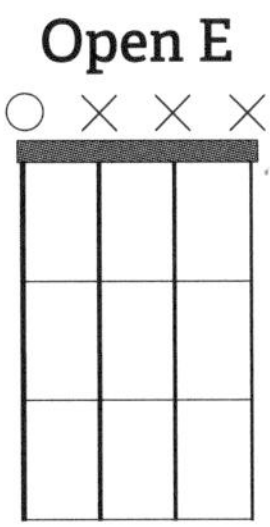

1 2 3 4

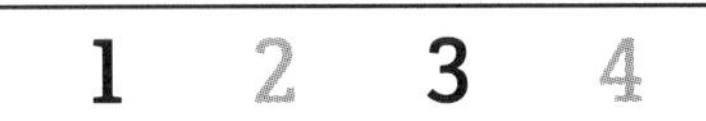

Now, try the activity with two more notes:

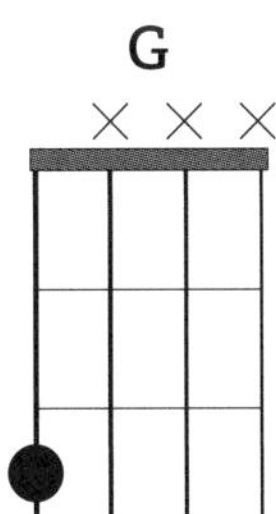

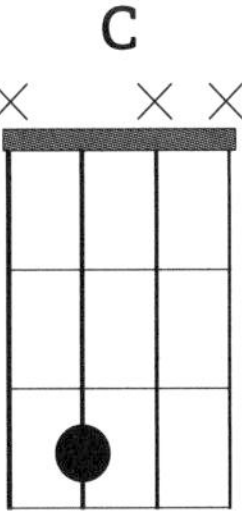

Improvisation: Two-Note Groove 

The two notes shown here can be used to play a groove:

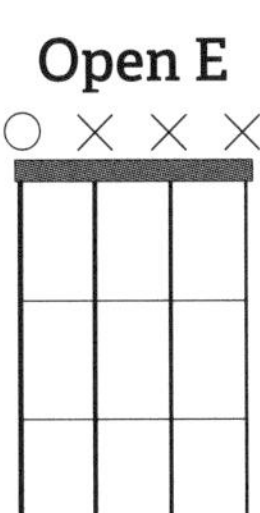

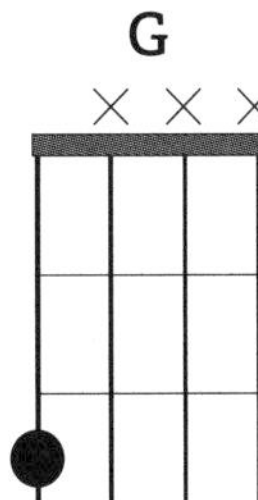

Practice playing these two notes in a variety of ways by mixing up the rhythm and order. Here are some ideas for improvisation:

- Start by playing the open note twice and switching to the G.
- Alternate between the two notes rapidly and then slowly. Then, try changing speeds.
- Focus on rhythm and lock in with the Jam Track.
- Play a rhythm on just the E, and then repeat that rhythm on the G.

Music Theory: The Song Chart

One way music is written is with a **lead sheet**. A lead sheet tells a musician what the chords of a song are. The lead sheet example below has four **measures** (or **bars**), which are divided by vertical lines (**bar lines**). Each measure is made up of four beats, shown by the diagonal lines, or **slashes** (/). You can play any four-beat picking patterns over those four beats. The measures are repeated over and over again, indicated by the **repeat bar** at the end.

The next part of the lead sheet is the notes. The song below uses a G for four beats (one measure), then an E for four beats, a C for four beats, and finally another E for four beats. For now, try just playing one note at the beginning of each measure.

CAN'T STOP THE FEELING!

Justin Timberlake

Another way music is written is with the names of notes or chords over the song lyrics. This type of chart doesn't tell you how many beats to play each note, but it shows you which lyrics you sing when the notes change. Play G when you sing "feeling" and switch to E on the word "bones." (Almost all charts include the full names of the chords for guitarists, keyboardists, and other musicians. As a bassist, just focus on the first letter of the chord name. When you see "Emi," just play the note E.)

```
                G               Emi
I've got this feeling inside my bones.

          C                       Emi
It goes electric, wavy when I turn it on.

                  G                  Emi
All through my city, all through my home,

              C                          Emi
We're flying up, no ceiling, when we in our zone.

             G                           Emi
I got that sunshine in my pocket, got that good soul in my feet.

             C                          Emi
I feel that hot blood in my body when it drops, ooh.

         G                    Emi
I can't take my eyes up off it, moving so phenomenally.

             C                          Emi
Room on lock the way we rock it, so don't stop.
```

Here are some other songs that use the same three notes, E, G, and C. In the first two songs, each note is played for eight beats.

WITHOUT YOU

David Guetta ft. Usher

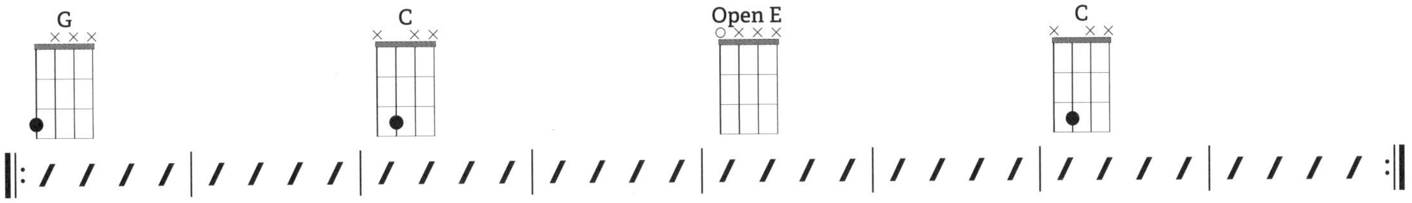

G C Open E C

|: / / / / | / / / / | / / / / | / / / / | / / / / | / / / / | / / / / | / / / / :|

1 2 3 4

G C Emi C
I can't win, I can't reign. I will never win this game without you, without you.

G C Emi C
I am lost, I am vain. I will never be the same without you, without you.

G C Emi C
I won't run, I won't fly. I will never make it by without you, without you.

G C Emi C
I can't rest, I can't fight. All I need is you and I, without you, without you.

To count the rhythm in this next song, say "1, 2 and, 3, 4 and." Pick on the numbers and on the "ands," shown by "+" symbols in the notation.

SEND MY LOVE (TO YOUR NEW LOVER)

Adele

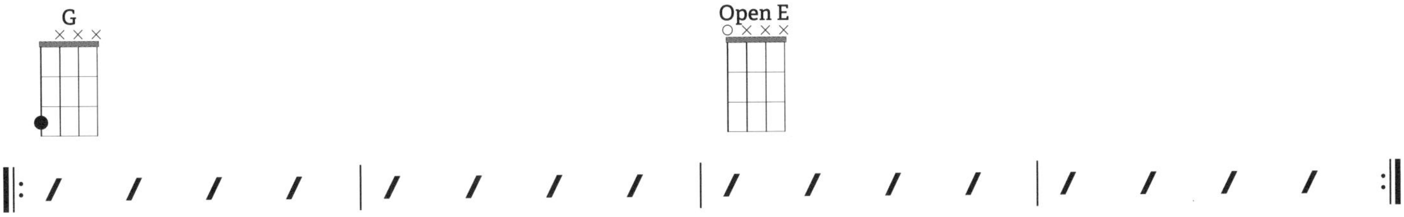

G Open E

|: / / / / | / / / / | / / / / | / / / / :|

1 2 + 3 4 +

G Emi
This was all you, none of it me. You put your hands on, on my body and told me,
you told me you were ready

G Emi
For the big one, for the big jump. I'd be your last love, everlasting, you and me.
That was what you told me.

G Emi
I'm giving you up, I've forgiven it all. You set me free.

G
Send my love to your new lover, treat her better.

Emi
We've gotta let go of all of our ghosts. We both know we ain't kids no more.

G
Send my love to your new lover, treat her better.

Emi
We've gotta let go of all of our ghosts.
We both know we ain't kids no more.

In this song, the E and C notes are played for two beats each, and then G is played for four beats.

WAKE ME UP

Avicii ft. John Legend

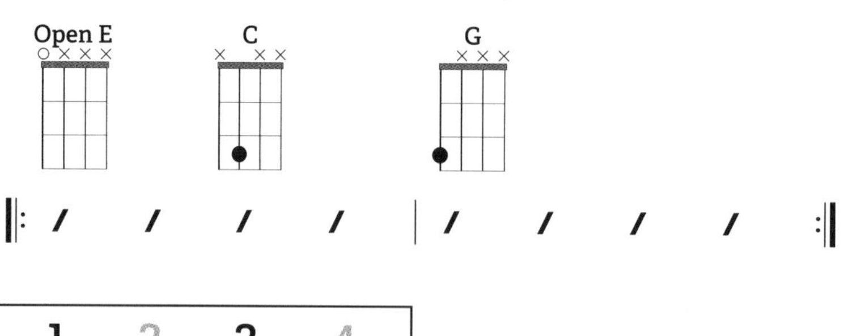

1 2 3 4

Emi C G
Feeling my way through the darkness,

Emi C G
Guided by a beating heart.

Emi C G
I can't tell where the journey will end,

Emi C G
But I know where to start.

Emi C G
They tell me I'm too young to understand.

Emi C G
They say I'm caught up in a dream.

Emi C G
Well, life will pass me by if I don't open up my eyes.

Emi C G
Well, that's fine by me.

Emi C G
So wake me up when it's all over,

Emi C G
When I'm wiser and I'm older.

Emi C G
All this time I was finding myself

Emi C G
And I didn't know I was lost.

Composition: E, C, G

Use E, C, and G to create your own song. Place the notes in the song chart below in any order you'd like. Then, choose any of the rhythms you have used so far to play those notes.

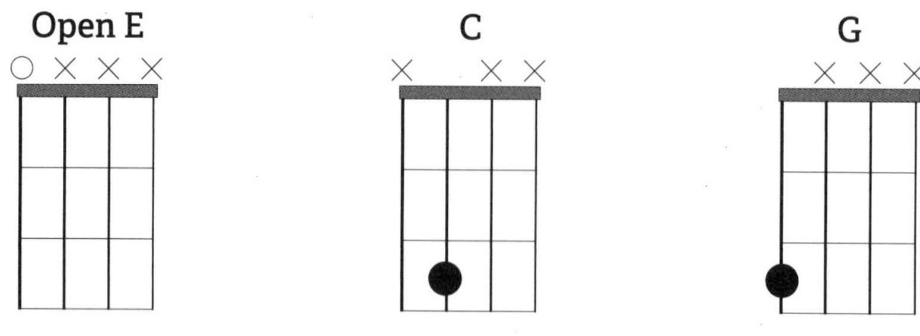

Bass Notes:

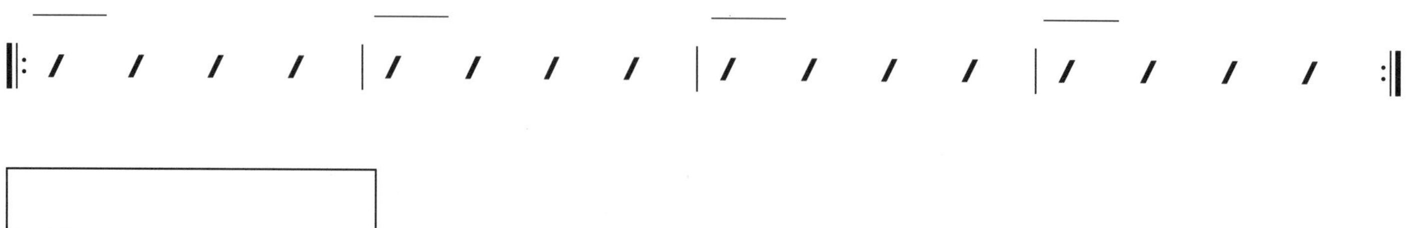

Full Band Song: I GOTTA FEELING

The Black Eyed Peas

Form of Recording: Intro–Chorus–Verse–Chorus–Verse–Chorus

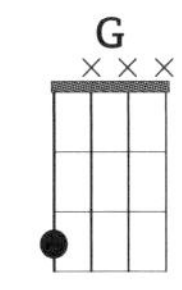

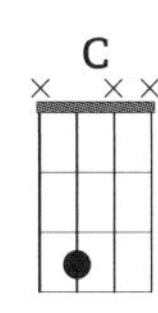

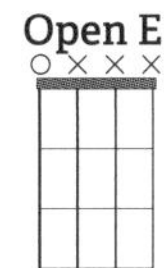

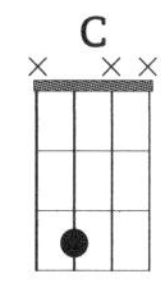

||: / / / / | / / / / | / / / / | / / / / | / / / / | / / / / | / / / / | / / / / :||

Use this rhythm for the Chorus: **1 2 3 4**

And use this rhythm for the Verse. To count this rhythm, say, "1 and, 2 and, 3 and, 4 and." Pick on the numbers and on the "ands," shown by "+" symbols in the notation. **1 + 2 + 3 + 4 +**

CHORUS

G **C**
I gotta feeling that tonight's gonna be a good night,

Emi **C**
That tonight's gonna be a good night, that tonight's gonna be a good, good night.

VERSE

G **C**
Tonight's the night, let's live it up. I got my money, let's spend it up.

Emi **C**
Go out and smash it, like, oh my God. Jump off that sofa, let's get, get off.

VERSE

G **C**
I know that we'll have a ball if we get down and go out and just lose it all.

Emi **C**
I feel stressed out, I wanna let go. Let's go way out, spaced out, and losing all control.

VERSE

G **C**
Fill up my cup, Mazel Tov! Look at her dancing, just take it off.

Emi
Let's paint the town, we'll shut it down.

C
Let's burn the roof, and then we'll do it again.

Going Beyond: Singing and Playing

An important skill for a musician playing popular music is to not only play songs, but also to sing along. Here are a few tips for singing and playing:

- Make sure you have learned the bass part well enough to play it without thinking about changing notes, then try speaking the lyrics in rhythm over it.
- Sing the lyrics while fretting the notes with just the left hand. Pick only when it's time to change notes.
- Don't worry too much about singing the correct pitches (notes) at this point; just practice the skill of doing two things at once.

SECTION 2

Playing Bass Lines: One-Note Song

Play the new note A and use the picking pattern below to play "Low Rider" by War.

LOW RIDER

War

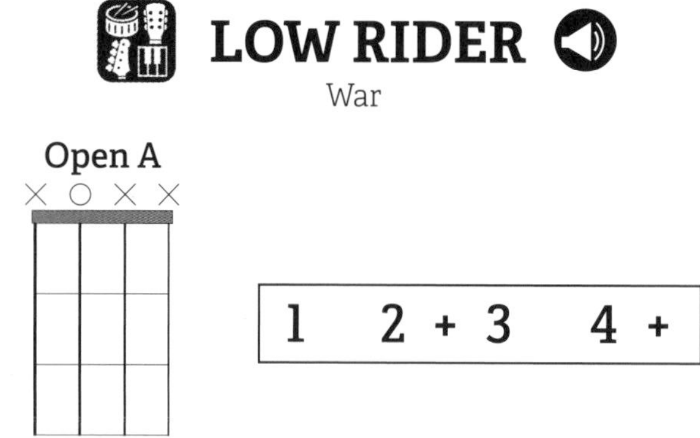

Music Theory: Reading Bass Tab

Tablature is another way to write music. It is used to write melodies and riffs. The tab **staff** has four lines, and each line represents a string. The thickest string on the bass is the lowest line on the tab.

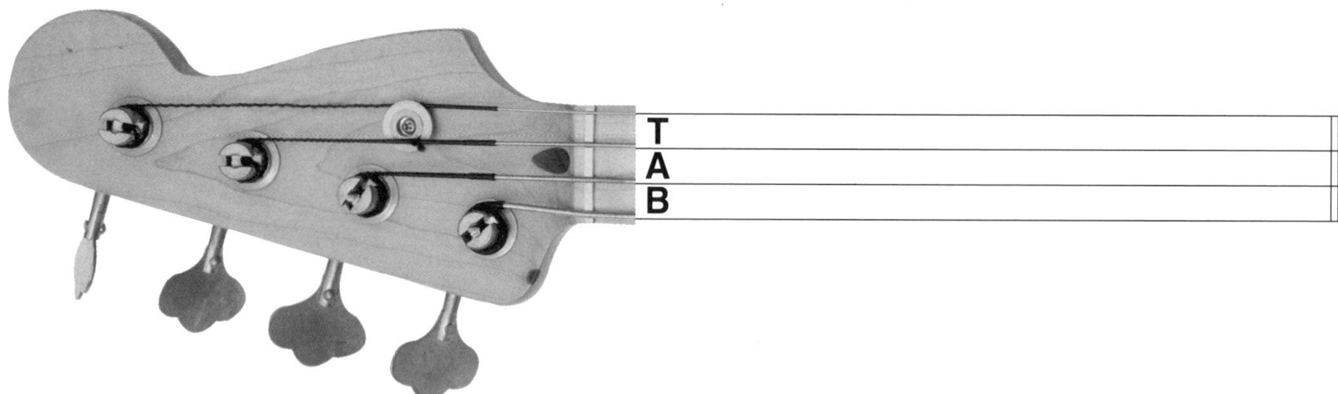

The next line up on the tab staff is the A string, which is the next string down on your bass guitar.

Here's a song you can use to practice playing the open E string evenly. Each "0" below tells you to pick the thickest string without holding down a fret with your left hand.

RUNNIN' WITH THE DEVIL

Van Halen

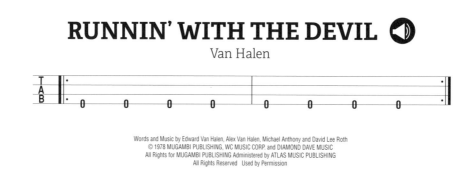

TAB: 0 0 0 0 | 0 0 0 0

Tablature can be used to learn new riffs. Numbers represent frets, not fingers. In the next example, the notes in the first measure are played on the 5th fret of the low E string; the notes in the second measure are played on the 3rd fret of the low E string, and so on.

Here are a couple riffs that just use the lowest string of the bass guitar. Listen to a recording of the songs for the rhythm.

25 OR 6 TO 4

Chicago

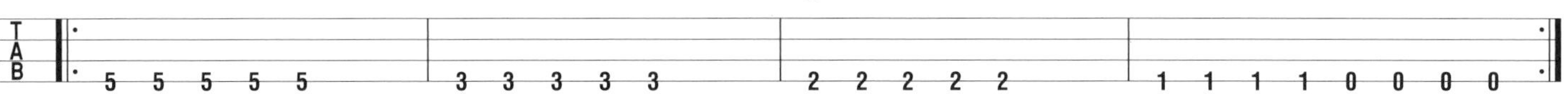

ONE NATION UNDER A GROOVE

Parliament Funkadelic

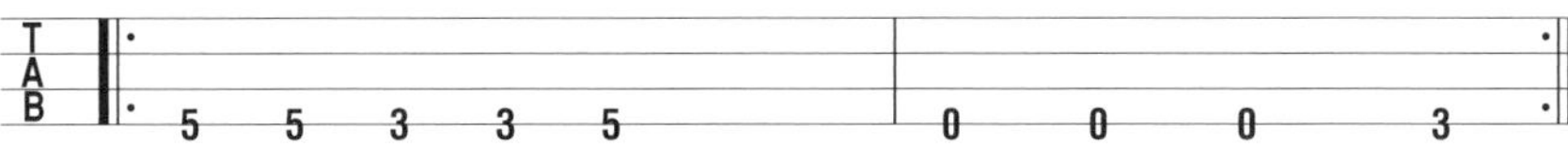

These next two examples also use the A string.

EX-FACTOR

Lauryn Hill

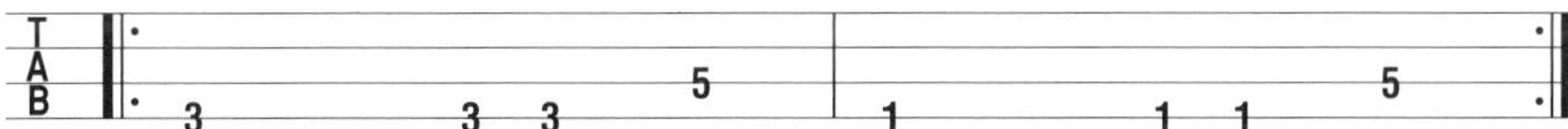

LET'S GROOVE

Earth, Wind & Fire

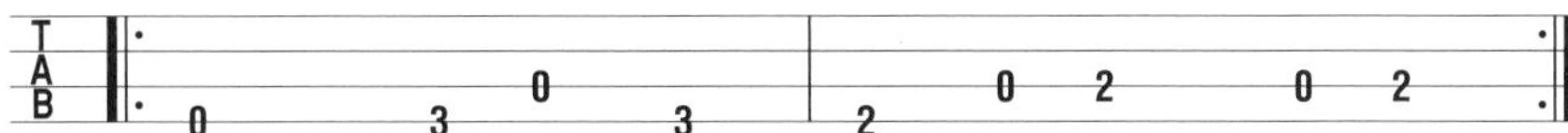

Instrument Technique: Strengthening Your Fingers

In order to be able to play a variety of riffs and grooves, you must have strong and flexible fingers. Try different combinations of fingerings along with the video. (Try finger 1 or finger 2 for the notes on the 2nd fret in the first example; try fingers 1 and 4, or fingers 2 and 4 for the second example.)

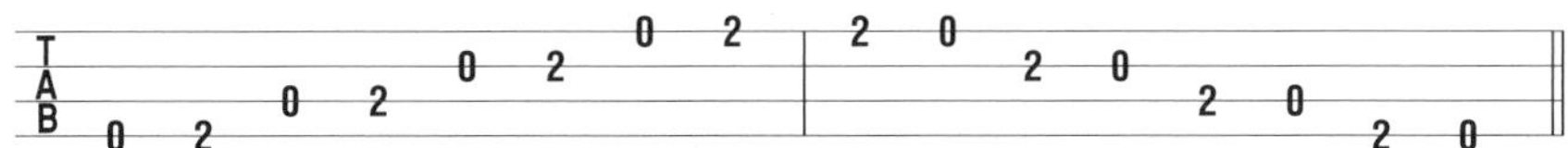

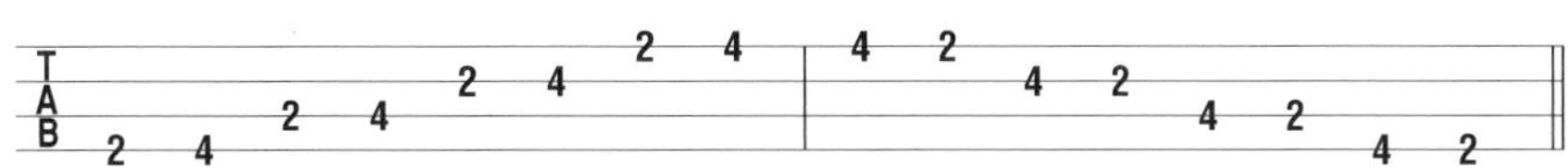

Now, in the next exercise, focus on getting a clear sound out of each note while playing along with the Jam Track.

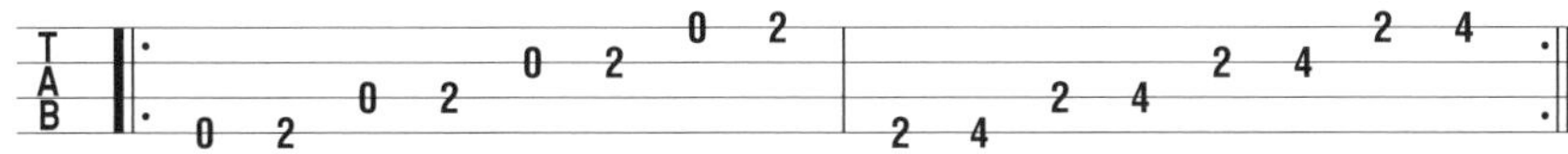

Instrument Technique: Muting Strings

The length of a bass note can change the feel of a song. You can change the length of a bass note by **muting** it. To mute a note, lightly touch the string with your right or left hand to stop the string from vibrating. Try playing the notes in "Shout" by the Isley Brothers both muted and unmuted:

SHOUT

The Isley Brothers

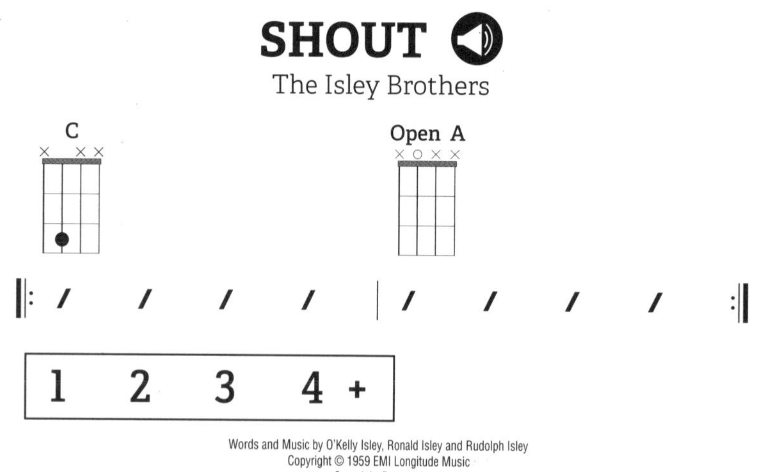

Improvisation: Four-Note Groove

You can expand the two-note groove to four notes by playing the same frets on the next string. Try improvising using these four notes:

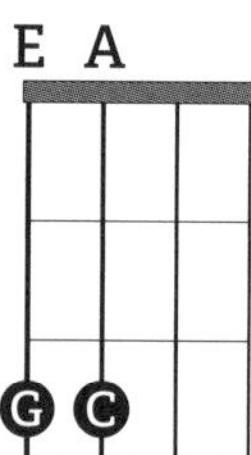

Here are a few examples of some bass grooves using the four notes, E, G, A, and C:

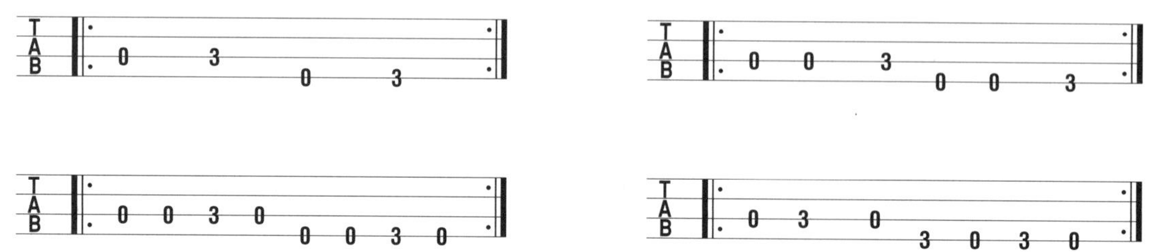

Music Theory: Whole Notes and Half Notes

In each measure of music so far, you have counted four beats. If you play a note once and let it ring for four beats, it lasts the whole measure. That is called a **whole note**. If it is cut in half, it becomes two **half notes**. Each whole note is four beats long, and each half note is two beats long.

Below, whole and half notes in traditional notation are shown along with their corresponding picking pattern.

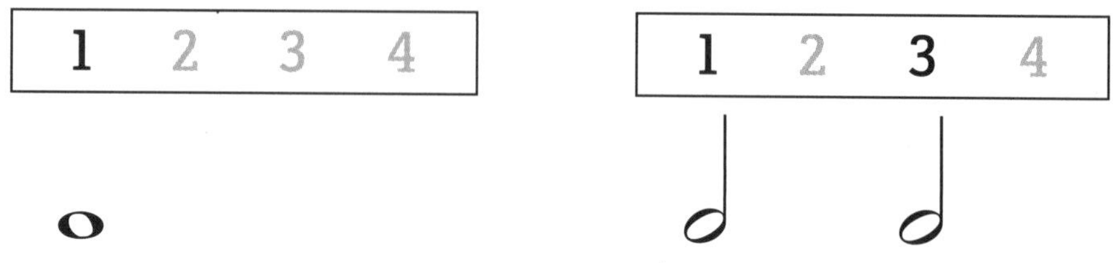

Full Band Song: HEATHENS

Twenty One Pilots

Form of Recording: Chorus–Verse–Chorus–Verse–Chorus–Chorus

Using traditional notation and note diagrams, you can read and play the Chorus of "Heathens" by Twenty One Pilots.

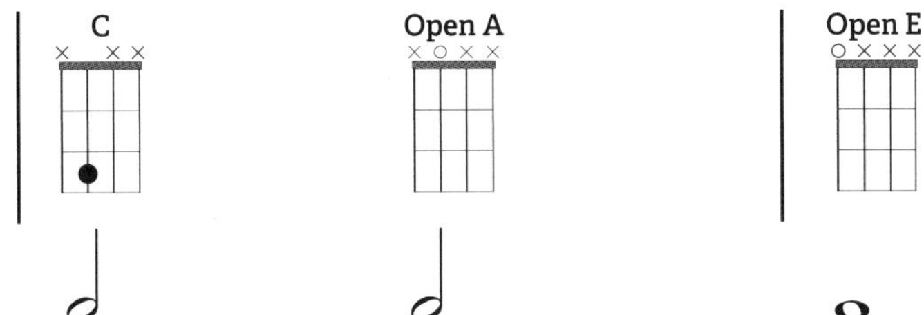

And here is the full song shown with slashes and note diagrams, as well as the chord and lyric chart below. In addition to the full Jam Track for this song, there are also two separate Jam Tracks for the Chorus and Verse looped so you can practice them individually.

Notice that the Verse includes a new note, B. This note is played on the 2nd fret of the 3rd string.

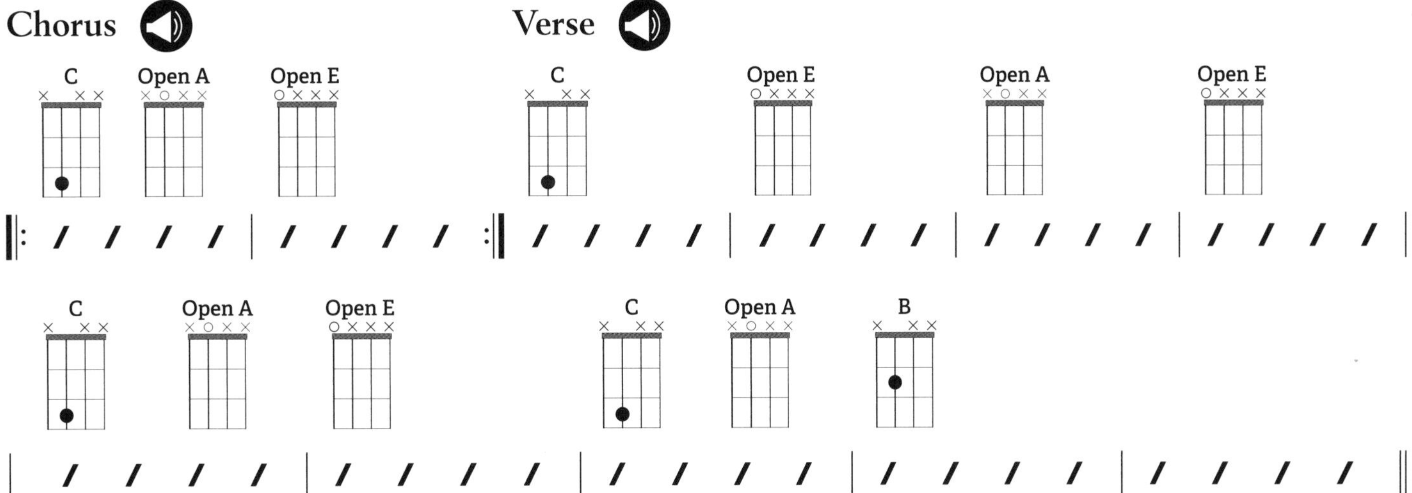

CHORUS

C All my friends are **Ami** heathens, take it **E** slow. **C** Wait for them to ask **Ami** you who you **E** know.

Please **C** don't make any **Ami** sudden **E** moves. You **C** don't know the half **Ami** of the **E** abuse.

VERSE

C Welcome to the room of people who have rooms of people
that they **Emi** loved one day docked away.

Ami Just because we check the guns at the door doesn't mean
our **Emi** brains will change from hand grenades.

C You'll never know the **Ami** psychopath sitting next to **Emi** you.
You'll never know the murderer sitting next to you.

C You'll think, "How'd I **Ami** get here, sitting next **B** to you?"
But after all I've said, please don't forget.

SECTION 3

Instrument Technique: Chromatic Riffs

In this next tab example, use a different finger to play each different fret. When we move like this from one fret to the next in an upward or downward line, it is called **chromatic**. If you need to, you can move your hand up and down on the neck.

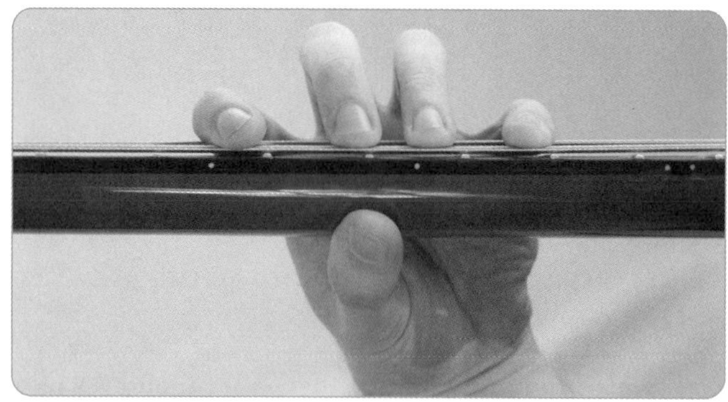

Now, check out your chromatic skills with this heavy Led Zeppelin riff. Listen to the original recording to hear the rhythms.

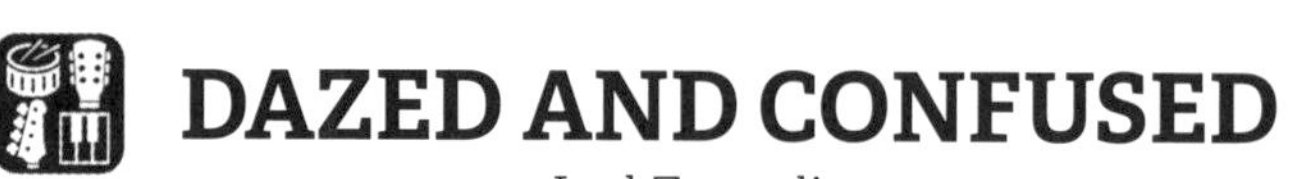

DAZED AND CONFUSED

Led Zeppelin

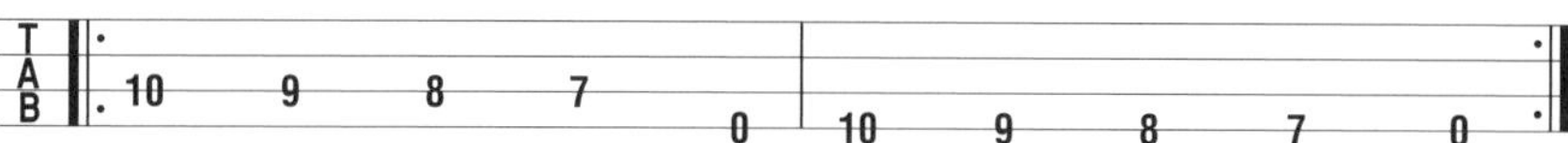

Or, you can play this riff like this.

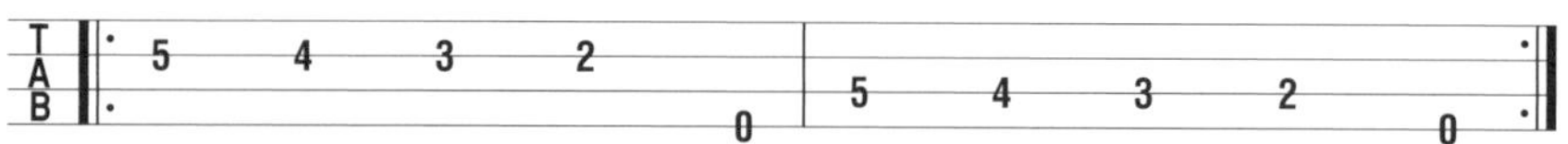

Playing Bass Lines: D

Using the notes A and D, you can play a variety of songs.

IMAGINE

John Lennon

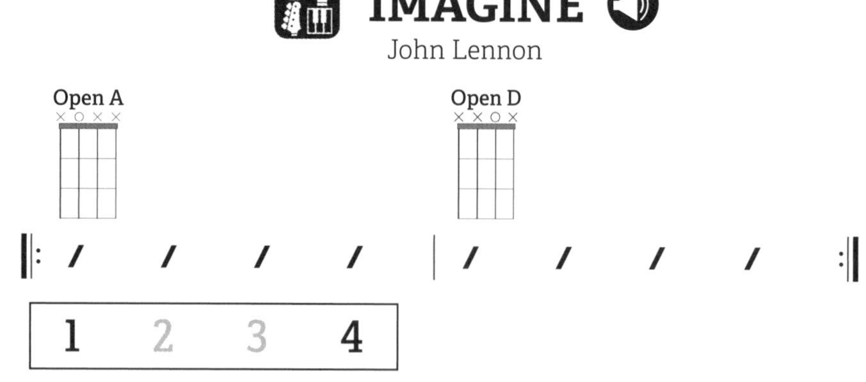

A **D** **A** **D**
Imagine there's no heaven. It's easy if you try.

A **D** **A** **D**
No hell below us. Above us only sky.

A **D** **A** **D**
Imagine there's no countries. It isn't hard to do.

A **D** **A** **D**
Nothing to kill or die for, and no religion, too.

BEST DAY OF MY LIFE

The American Authors

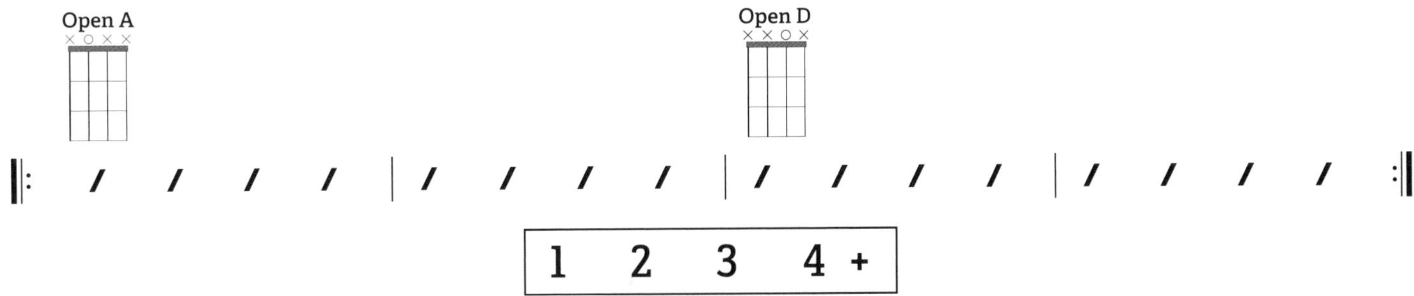

A
I had a dream so big and loud, I jumped so high I touched the clouds.

D
Whoa-o-o-o-o-oh. Whoa-o-o-o-o-oh.

A
I stretched my hands out to the sky. We danced with monsters through the night.

D
Whoa-o-o-o-o-oh. Whoa-o-o-o-o-oh.

A   **D**
Wo-o-o-o-oo! This is gonna be the best day of my life, my life.

A   **D**
Wo-o-o-o-oo! This is gonna be the best day of my life, my life.

Music Theory: Quarter and Eighth Notes

Half notes can be broken into two **quarter notes**. Each quarter note gets one beat.

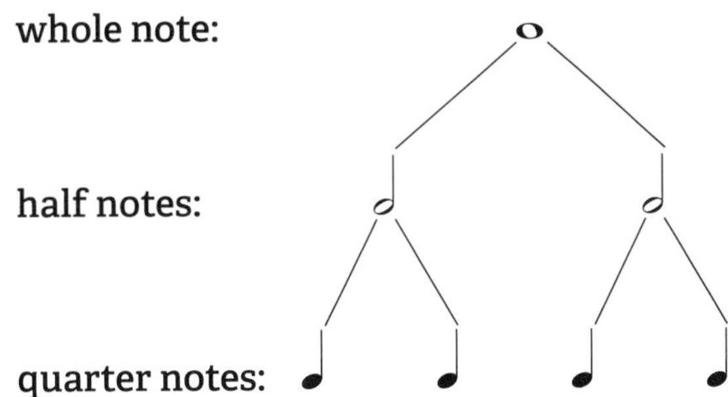

Playing and Resting

You can also use a **rest** when you want to stop the strings from ringing and leave some space. Try this while switching between the notes A and D. A rest means "count, but don't play." Each **quarter rest** gets one beat.

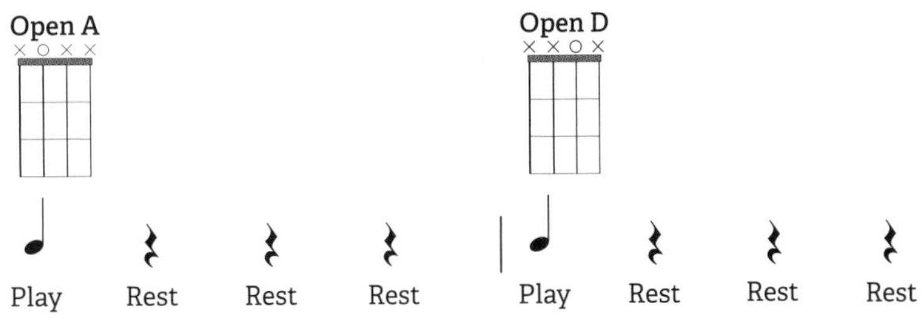

Quarter notes can be broken into **eighth notes**. Each eighth note gets a half of a beat.

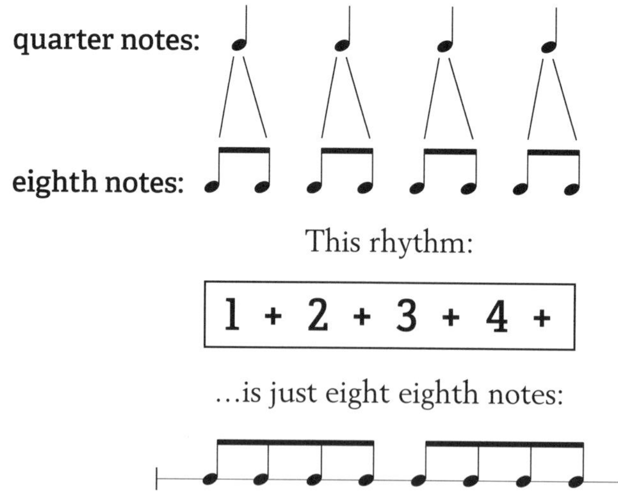

These picking patterns combine quarter notes and eighth notes in different combinations. Try picking and counting them.

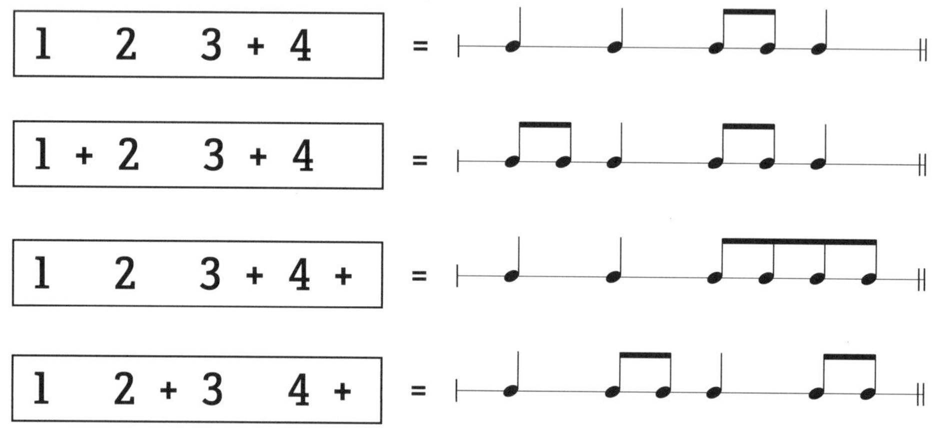

Improvisation: Creating a Groove

Bass players don't often take solos, but they almost never stop playing, even when another band member is soloing. The key to being a great bass player is to lay down a solid groove for the other bandmates to sing or play with.

Here are a few basic grooves to get you started. Feel free to create variations on these to compose your own grooves.

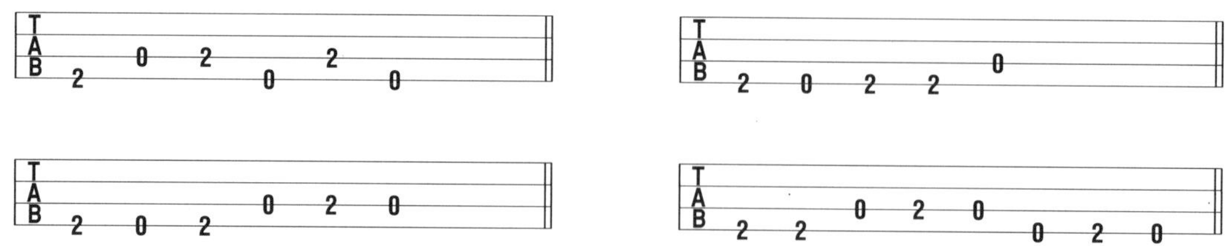

Composition: Compose a Riff

Using the notes we've already learned, try creating your own bass riff. Here is a sample two-bar riff:

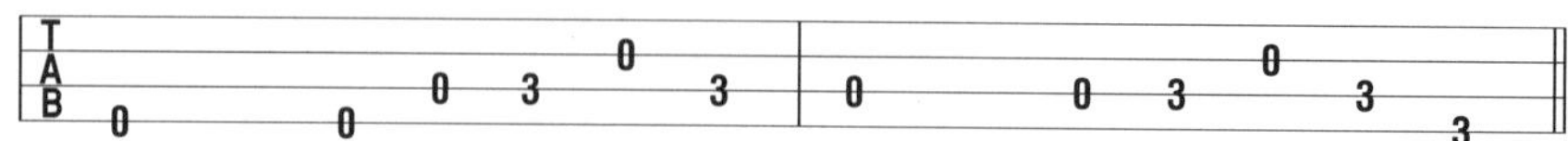

Write your original riff here:

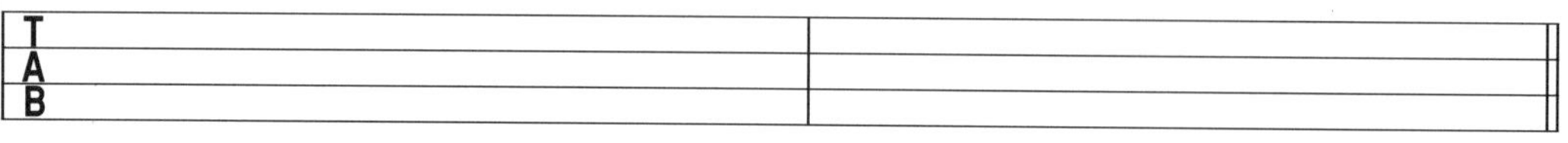

SECTION 4

Instrument Technique: Some New Riffs

Here are some bass riffs that use multiple strings. Listen to the following songs to get a sense of the rhythms.

UNDERNEATH IT ALL

No Doubt

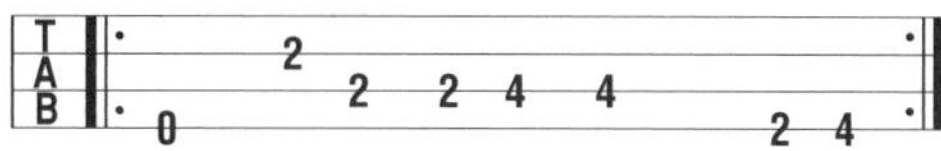

WANNABE

Spice Girls

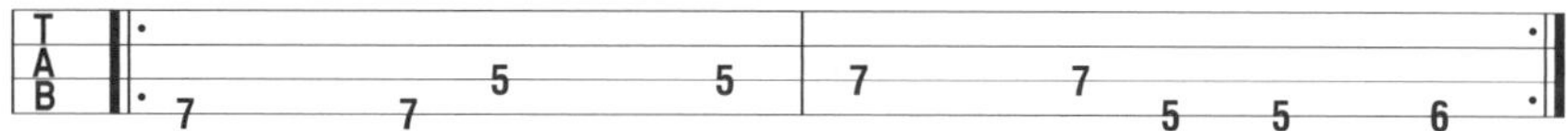

For these next two riffs, focus on changing strings. If you're playing fingerstyle for "Under Pressure," alternate your right-hand index and middle fingers to play the fast part.

UNDER PRESSURE

Queen ft. David Bowie

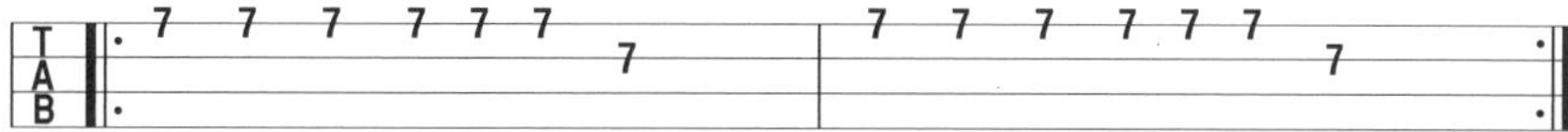

SEVEN NATION ARMY

The White Stripes

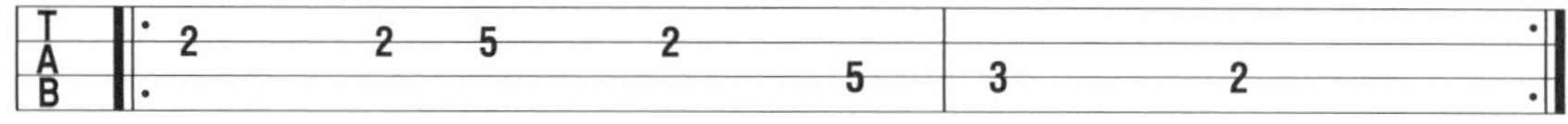

Instrument Technique: Muting Notes

As a bass player, you serve both a rhythmic (like a drummer) and harmonic (like a guitarist or keyboardist) role in a band. It's very important that you play in time. To help make your notes last only as long as you want them, you can **mute** them with either your left or right hand. To mute an open string, touch the string lightly to stop the vibration; you can do this with your left hand, right hand, or both. To mute fretted notes, lift the finger you're fretting with to stop the string from vibrating. Try muting in these examples. If you listen to the original recordings, you can hear these notes are played short.

T A B: 0 0 0 0 | 2 2 2 2 2

Composition: Writing Lyrics

Here are three steps you can take to write your own song lyrics:

1. Pick a theme. Lyrics can be easy to write when you have something you want to say. Think of something you care about and write based on that, such as friends, family, hobbies, or dreams.
2. Choose two words that rhyme, such as "great" and "late," or "thrill" and "chill." Then, choose another pair.
3. Turn your words into sentences. Try to speak the words in rhythm and sing them with the Jam Track. Here is an example of a verse for a song written about songwriting:

Writing lyrics is so fun, can be done by any - one.

| / / / / | / / / / |

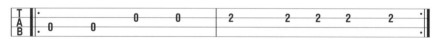

Think of what to write a - bout; play some chords, and sing or shout!

| / / / / | / / / / ||

Full Band Song: STIR IT UP

Bob Marley & the Wailers

Form of Recording: Intro–Chorus–Verse–Chorus–Verse–Chorus

With this Full Band Song, you can focus on just the root notes (the note diagrams) or play the tab.

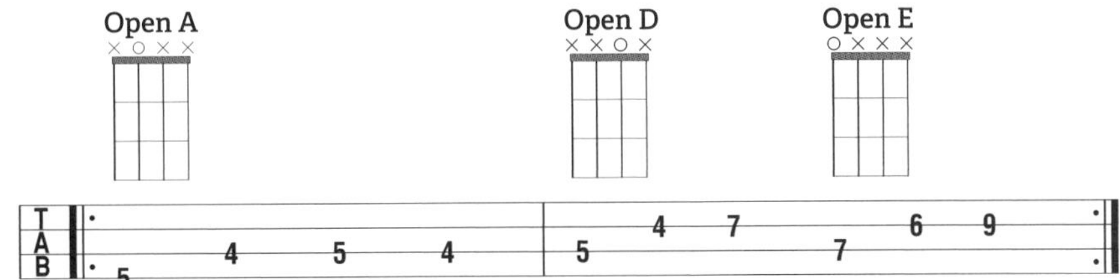

CHORUS

A D E A D E
Stir it up. Little darlin', stir it up. Come on, baby.

A D E A D E
Come on and stir it up. Little darlin', stir it up. O-oh!

VERSE

A D
It's been a long, long time, yeah (stir it, stir it, stir it together).

E A D E
Since I got you on my mind (ooh-ooh-ooh-ooh).

A D E
Now you are here (stir it, stir it, stir it together). I said, it's so clear.

A D E
To see what we could do, baby (ooh-ooh-ooh-ooh). Just me and you.

SECTION 5

Instrument Technique: Muted Note Review & Rhythms

Play these bass lines, keeping the length of each note in mind. Having control over the length of each note is an important skill for a bass player. Also, do you notice how these songs all use almost all the same notes, but are different genres?

From this point on, standard staff notation will be included with the tabs. Use this to begin familiarizing yourself with where the notes are on the staff. If you see any symbols or rhythms you don't understand, continue listening to the original recordings to hear the rhythms. You'll learn more about music reading as you continue through the Modern Band program.

HYPNOTIZE

The Notorious BIG

MY OWN WORST ENEMY

Lit

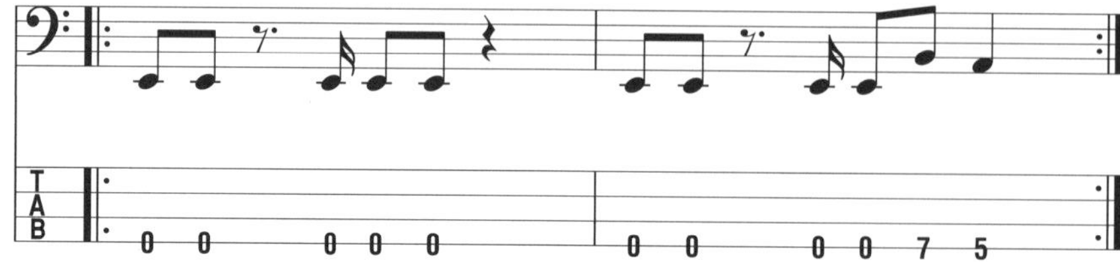

Music Theory: Notes, Chords, and Scales

All music is made up of the notes of the musical alphabet. All the riffs and chords you have been playing are made up of these individual notes. There are seven **natural notes**: A–B–C–D–E–F–G.

Chords are a combination of notes played together. Bass players rarely play chords. But it is important to know that other musicians, such as guitarists and keyboardists, often do.

A **scale** is a series of notes. The notes we've been using to improvise grooves all part of one scale or another. We will learn more about this later in the book.

The combination of notes, chords, and scales put to rhythm defines all the music we experience.

Playing Bass Lines: Drum and Bass

Play this next example with a drummer.

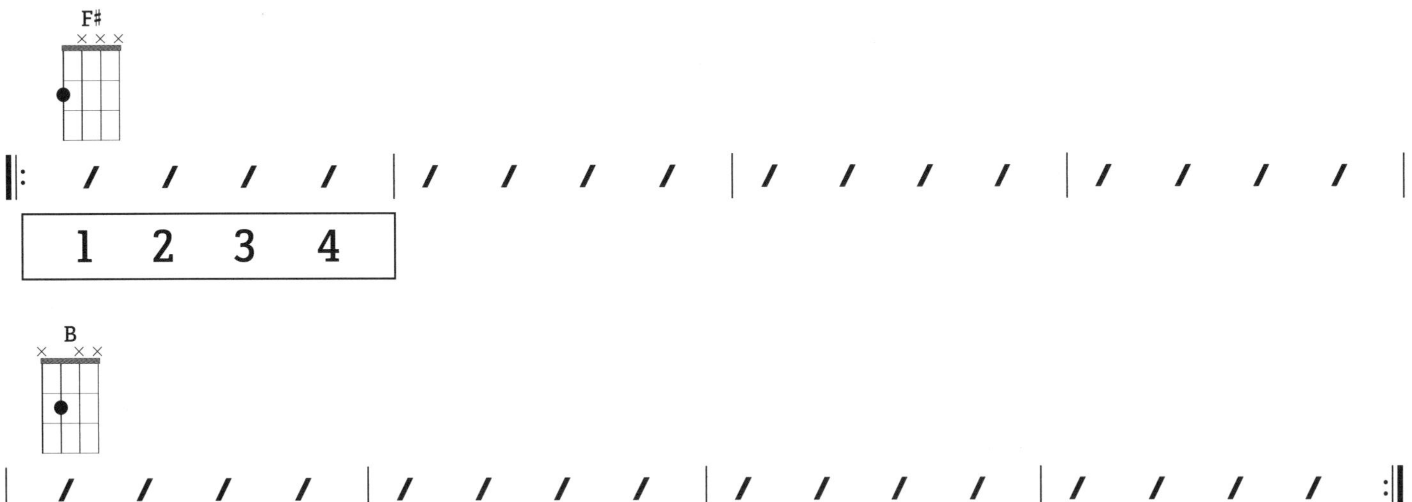

Notice how both the bass guitar and bass drum play on all four downbeats in this groove. Since it is the same rhythm, make sure your playing lines up exactly with the bass drum.

Both the bass drum and bass guitar are called "bass" because they sound low in pitch.

For this exercise, counting is included between the standard notation and the tab.

In both measures of this example from Weezer's "Say It Ain't So," the second note of each measure lands on the "and" between beats 2 and 3, rather than on the beat.

SAY IT AIN'T SO

Weezer

In this example, there is an eight-beat groove (two measures of four beats each). Count along and be sure to notice which notes are played on the "and" and which are played on the downbeats.

FREE FALLIN'

Tom Petty

1 (2) + (3) (4) 1 + (2) + (3) (4)

In a great band, all the musicians pay close attention to what their bandmates are playing. For bassists, listening to the drummer is especially important. Together, the bass and drums tell the rest of the band important information about tempo, rhythm, style, and note lengths. In this section, you've been encouraged to practice with a drummer, and should be starting to notice some examples of the bass-drum connection in music. With that in mind, let's try two more examples.

DOO WOP (THAT THING)

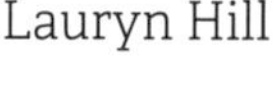

Lauryn Hill

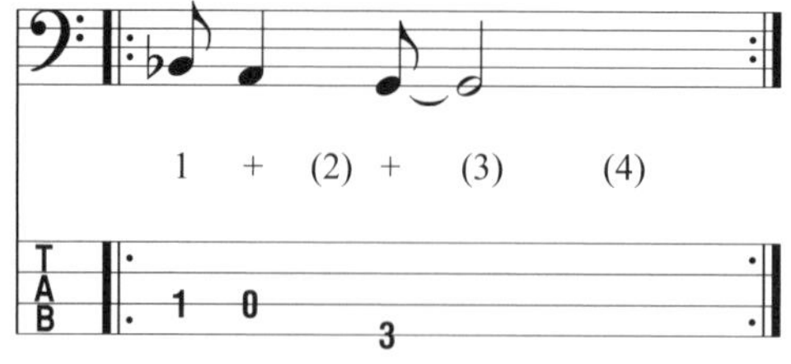

YOU KNOW I'M NO GOOD

Amy Winehouse

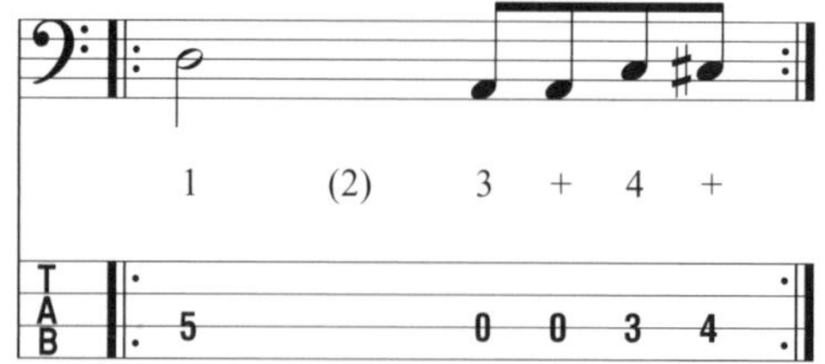

Composition: Mastering the Grid

Now that you've played several examples of grooves where the bass drum and bass guitar play the same rhythms, try writing some of your own. First, look at every eighth-note option below. Then, create riffs in the empty tab below using different rhythm patterns and any notes of your choice. If a drummer is available, practice the new rhythms together.

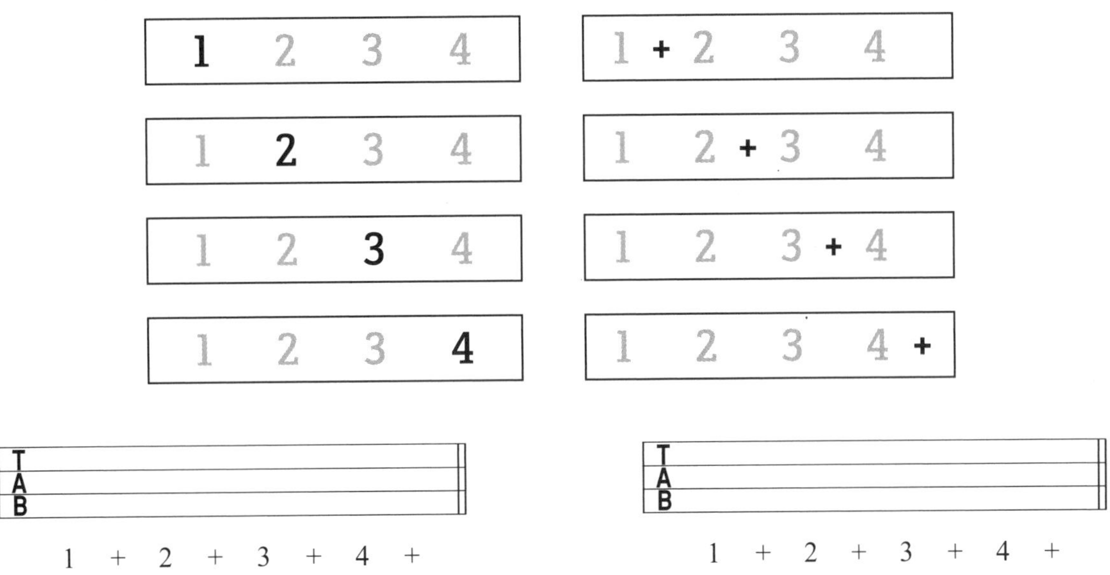

Drummers don't only use the bass drum to line up with the bassist. Work with your drummer to find drum sounds that work best with the notes and rhythms that you're playing. For example, you may want the lower notes you play to be matched with a bass drum or other lower-pitched drum, and the higher notes with a higher-pitched drum (like a snare drum). Try creating a few more riffs together with that in mind.

As you listen to more music—with the drum-bass relationship in mind—you'll notice that a lot of the rhythms won't line up *exactly*, but rather, the bass and drums work together to emphasize, or **accent**, certain notes.

Improvisation: Full Minor Pentatonic Scale

The first scale you'll learn is the **minor pentatonic scale.**

A Minor Pentatonic

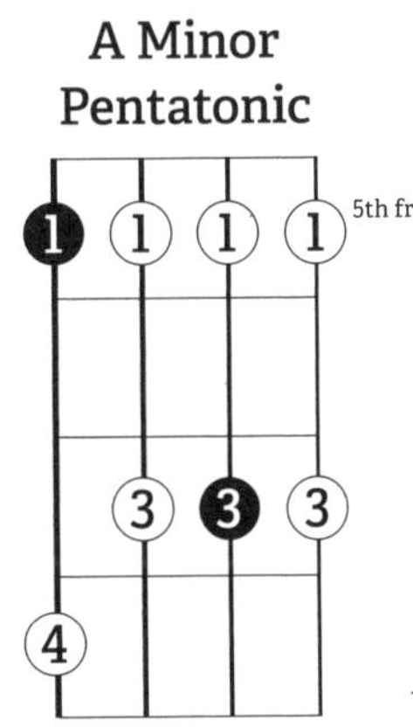

The **tonic**, or **root**, is the note a scale or chord is named after. For this scale, starting at the 5th fret on string 4, the tonic is A. Both darkened notes in the diagram are A notes.

This scale sounds good with songs that have a bluesy or funky sound, like "Low Rider" by War.

A fun way to practice this scale is to create bass lines using notes from the scale. Practice playing up and down the scale, using different rhythms. Next, try skipping different notes of the scale. Finally, try playing some notes long and some notes short. Many bass lines are based on the pentatonic scale.

Here are a few riffs that use the pentatonic scale.

LARGER THAN LIFE

Backstreet Boys

BILLIE JEAN

Michael Jackson

THRILLER

Michael Jackson

Try to make some of your own riffs with the minor pentatonic scale:

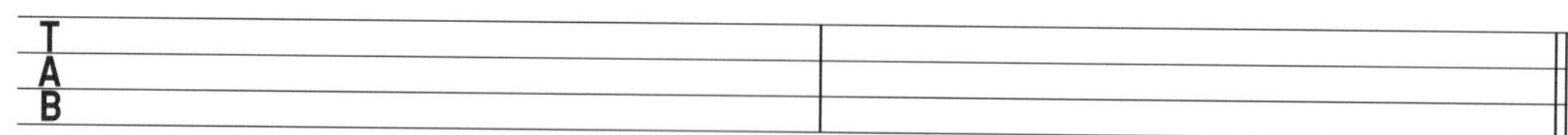

SECTION 6

Playing Bass Lines: One-Note Song

Here's a song that uses just one chord. You can practice with either a recording of the song or with your whole band. It's a great exercise for rehearsing even and steady eighth notes. If you're playing with a drummer, it's another great opportunity to practice locking in together.

 LAND OF A THOUSAND DANCES 

Wilson Pickett

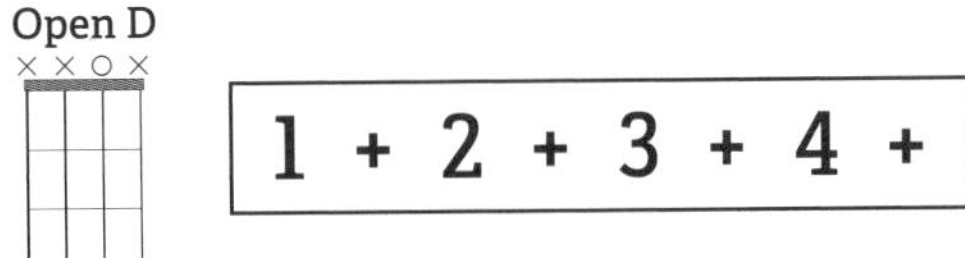

Instrument Technique: Changing the Rhythm

A bass player can change the feel of a song by playing different rhythms, just as a drummer can change the feel of a song by changing up their drumbeat.

Play these different rhythms on the note A (as written), or any other single note of your choice.

Music Theory: The Music Staff

While tablature is useful for guitarists and bass guitarists, it doesn't translate to most other instruments. However, **standard staff notation** can be shared between different instruments.

Look at this bass line in tablature from a song you have already learned, "Heathens" by Twenty One Pilots.

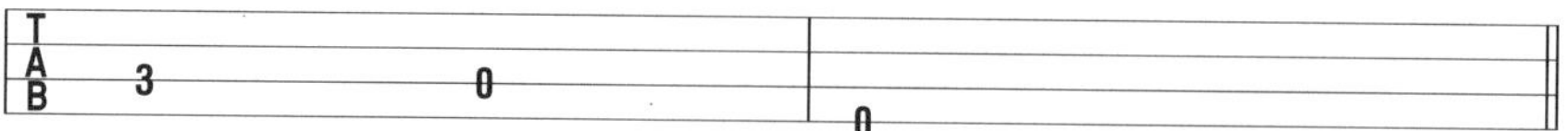

Every note on the bass has a place on the **music staff**. To start, look at a music staff, which is similar to a tab staff but with a few differences—there are five lines instead of four, and the lines *do not* refer to strings.

The next important feature on a staff is the **bass clef**. It assigns specific note names to the lines and spaces on the staff.

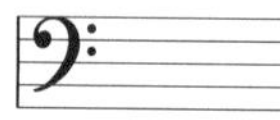

You have already seen note heads used with rhythms. Here they are placed on the staff in the lines and spaces to let the musician know which notes to play. The vertical placement of each note determines what note it is. Every number in the tab staff corresponds to *exactly* one place on a music staff.

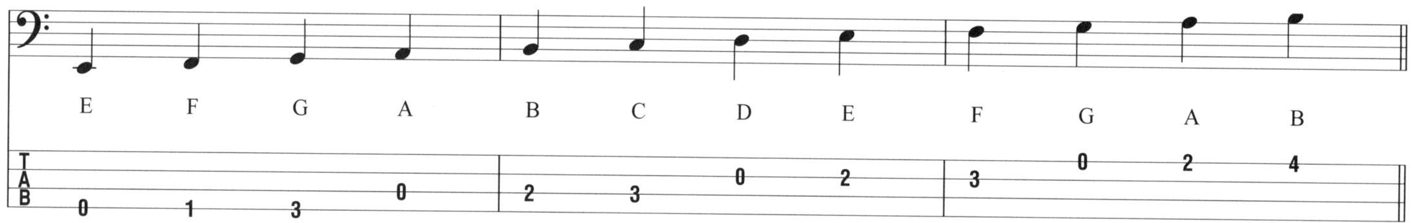

Using the tab and rhythms from "Heathens," we can now write the bass line in standard staff notation.

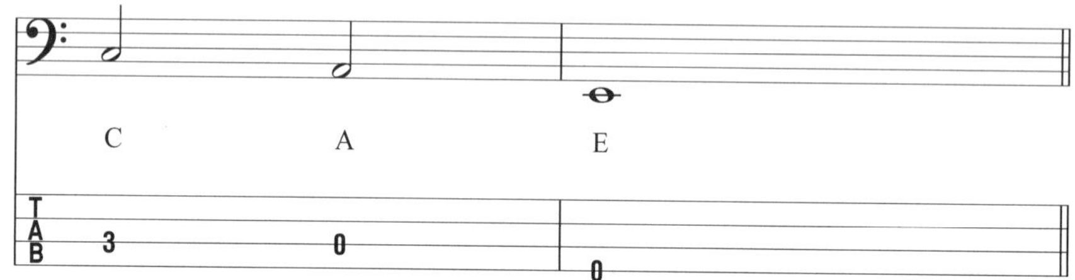

Play a few bass lines using traditional staff notation. The rhythms of some have been simplified to use only the rhythms covered so far. (The dot after the half note in measure 1 means to hold that note for three beats instead of two—and of course, the quarter note lasts for one beat.) Once you play them, write the tab showing how you played it.

BABA O'RILEY

The Who

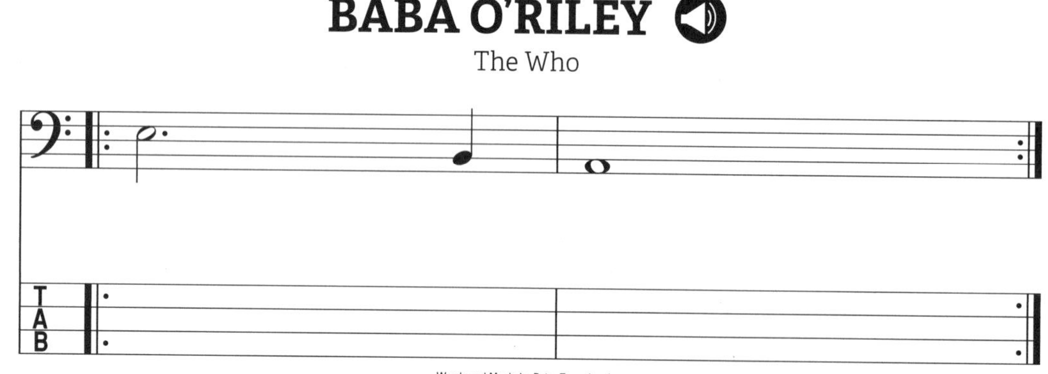

UNDER PRESSURE

Queen ft. David Bowie

LIVIN' ON A PRAYER

Bon Jovi

To play the next melody from "I Can't Help Myself (Sugar Pie, Honey Bunch)," we'll need to know the **eighth rest**: 𝄾. This rest takes the place of one eighth note. Combined with another eighth note or eighth rest, it makes up a full beat. Find a recording of the following song and listen to the intro to hear how the rhythm works with the notation.

I CAN'T HELP MYSELF (SUGAR PIE, HONEY BUNCH) 

The Four Tops

Full Band Song: SOMEONE LIKE YOU

Adele

Form of Recording: Intro–Verse–Pre-Chorus–Chorus–Verse–Pre-Chorus–Chorus–Bridge–Chorus

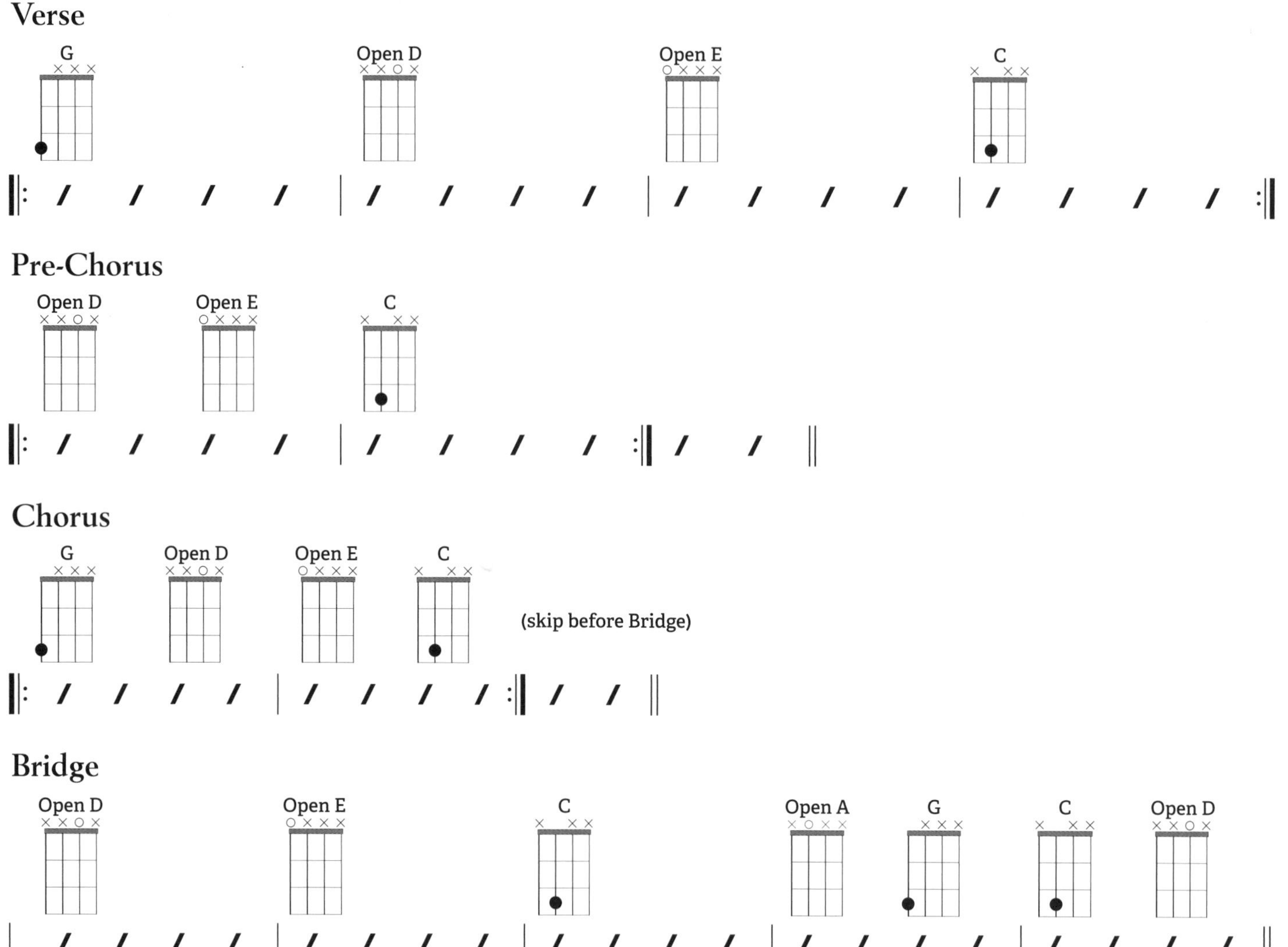

Verse/Bridge Rhythm Pattern

1	2	3	4

Chorus Rhythm Pattern

1	2	3	4

VERSE

G   D   Emi   C
I heard that you're settled down, that you found a girl and you're married now.

G   D   Emi   C
I heard that your dreams came true. Guess she gave you things I didn't give to you.

G   D   Emi   C
Old friend, why are you so shy? Ain't like you to hold back or hide from the light.

PRE-CHORUS

D   Emi   C
I hate to turn up out of the blue uninvited, but I couldn't stay away, I couldn't fight it.

D   Emi   C
I had hoped you'd see my face and that you'd be reminded that for me it isn't over.

CHORUS

G   D   Emi   C
Never mind, I'll find someone like you.

        G   D   Emi   C
I wish nothing but the best for you two.

G   D   Emi   C
Don't forget me, I beg. I'll remember you said,

               G   D   Emi   C
"Sometimes it lasts in love, but sometimes it hurts instead,

               G   D   Emi   C
Sometimes it lasts in love, but sometimes it hurts instead."

BRIDGE

D
Nothing compares, no worries or cares,

    Emi
Regrets and mistakes, they're memories made.

C   Ami   G   C   D
Who would have known how bittersweet this would taste?

SECTION 7

Playing Bass Lines: Rhythmic Patterns

Practice playing through these patterns while staying on the same note of your choice. Then, try changing the note for each pattern.

1 2 3 4	1 2 3 + 4	1 + 2 + 3 + 4 +
1 2 + 3 + 4 +	1 2 + 3 + 4	1 2 + 3 + 4 +

Composition: Introduction 

A lot of songs have an **introduction**. An introduction is often the instrumental section that happens before the vocalist begins. To compose an introduction, choose chords for each of the four bars below using the chords (notes) you know. Use the Jam Track to try out your ideas.

Then, choose a picking pattern:

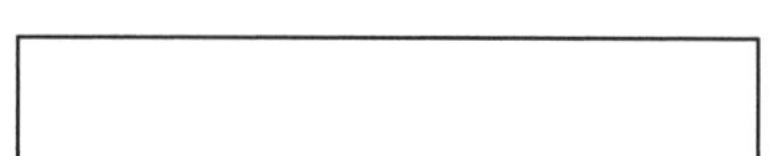

Now, add a riff to your introduction using this scale:

A Minor Pentatonic

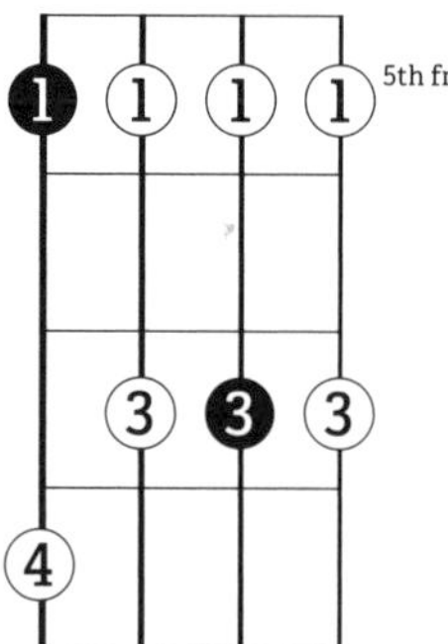

T
A
B

Full Band Song: OYE COMO VA

Santana

Form of Recording: Intro–Verse–Breakdown 1–Verse–Breakdown 1–Verse–Breakdown 1–Verse–Breakdown 2–Verse

As a bass player, you don't have to worry about playing chords. You should focus on playing just the root notes of each chord. This is most often the letter name of the chord.

The main riff of "Oye Como Va" by Santana uses the rhythm shown below. Counting the rhythm out loud is a great way to help you learn it. Play A for the first three notes, then switch to D for the last three. Or, if you want to play the exact bass line, follow the tab below. (Notice the note C on beat 4 of the second measure.)

Verse

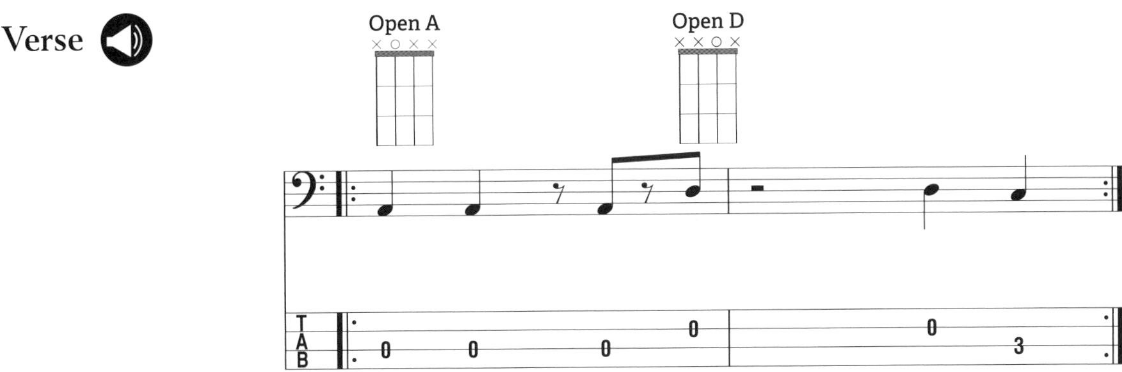

The following fill comes up periodically throughout the song. It happens first at the 30-second mark on the original recording.

Breakdown 1

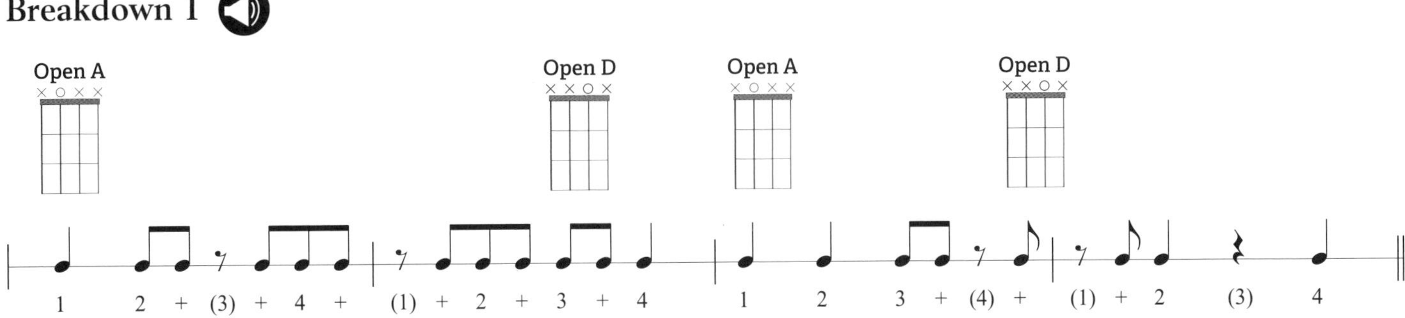

Here's the last section, which is played over an E chord. This shows up just twice in the song. It's played one time around the two-minute mark, and then later it's played twice. For this section, just use the note E.

Breakdown 2

Ami **D**
Oye como va, mi ritmo.

Ami **D**
Bueno pa gozar, mulata.

Ami **D**
Oye como va, mi ritmo.

Ami **D**
Bueno pa gozar, mulata.

SECTION 8

Instrument Technique: Two-String Riffs

One way to keep your fingers nimble is to learn more riffs. Here are a few more that focus on two strings:

COME AS YOU ARE

Nirvana

U CAN'T TOUCH THIS

MC Hammer

UPTOWN FUNK

Mark Ronson ft. Bruno Mars

Instrument Technique: Steady Eighth Notes

A bassist is just as important as a drummer when it comes to keeping time. When playing steady eighth notes, bassists often alternate between their index and middle finger. If you're using a pick, alternate between upstrokes and downstrokes.

Here are a few bass lines that have steady eighth notes:

U2

SUPERMASSIVE BLACK HOLE

Muse

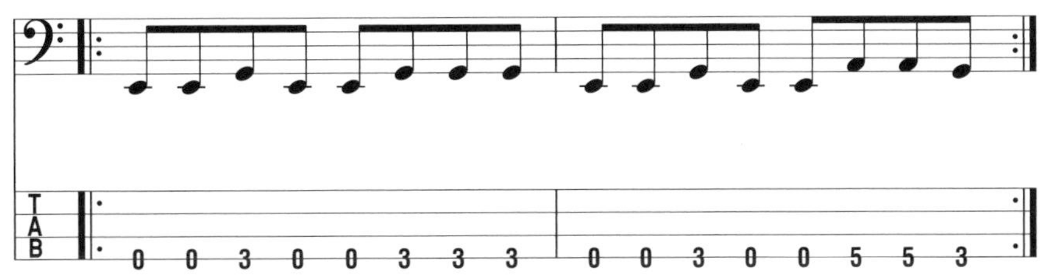

The Cranberries

Always practice these bass lines with the Jam Tracks or a metronome to make sure you're playing steady and in time.

Music Theory: Syncopated Patterns

These next patterns, in which upbeats are played after skipping downbeats, are called **syncopated** rhythms. To practice with the Jam Track, follow the rhythm of the bass drum and play an open E on beats 1 and the "and" of beat 2.

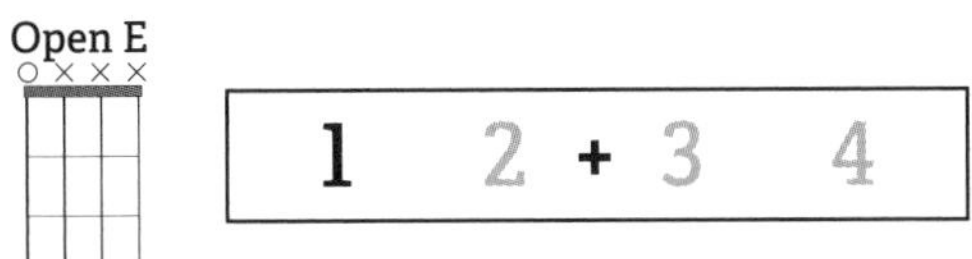

If you take that same pattern but change the notes (two per bar), you can play a few other songs:

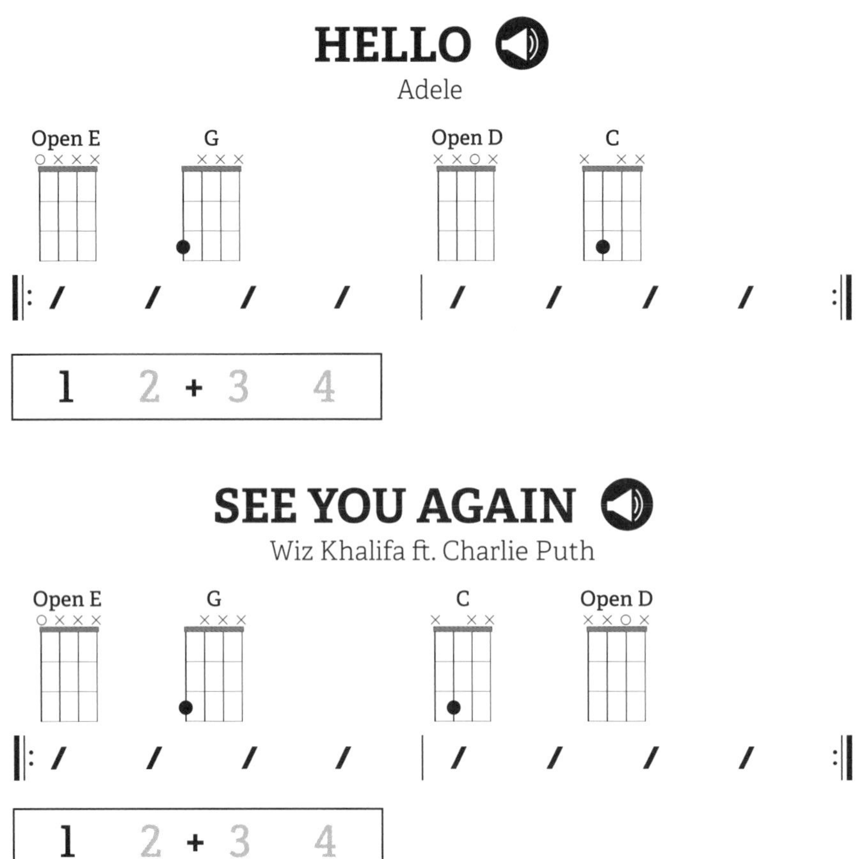

Playing Bass Lines: Reggae Bass

Keeping note length and stylistically appropriate rhythms in mind, you can play this reggae song by Bob Marley & the Wailers. Keeping the bass notes short is iconic of much reggae music.

5446, THAT'S MY NUMBER

The Maytals

Full Band Song: WAKA WAKA (THIS TIME FOR AFRICA)

Shakira

Form of Recording: Intro–Verse–Pre-Chorus–Chorus–Interlude–Verse–Pre-Chorus–Chorus–Bridge–Chorus

For this song, you will play the same notes for each section.

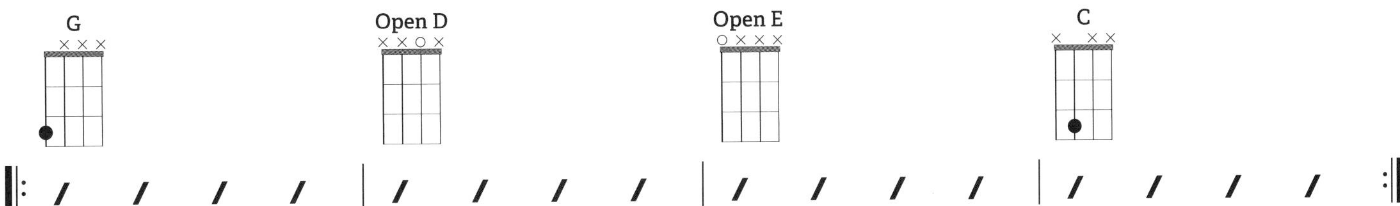

In the Intro, just play the note G using the following syncopated rhythm. This rhythm uses a **dotted eighth note** connected to a **sixteenth note**—which we haven't covered yet in this series. Use your ear to match the rhythm of the original recording.

During the Verse and Pre-Chorus, the bass can play whole notes.

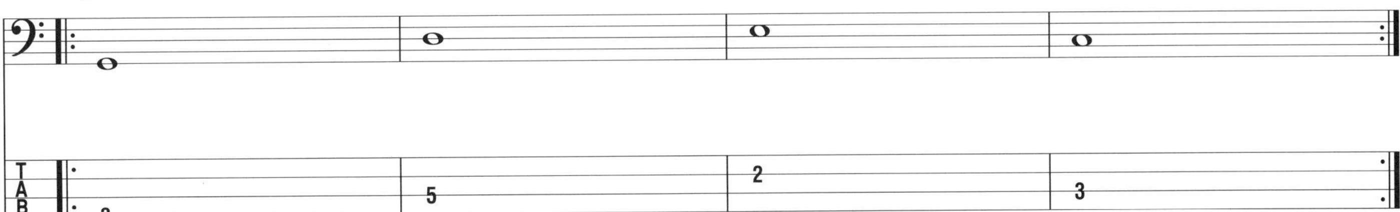

In the Chorus of the song, the bass line moves a bit more. Use the tab and notation below to learn the part.

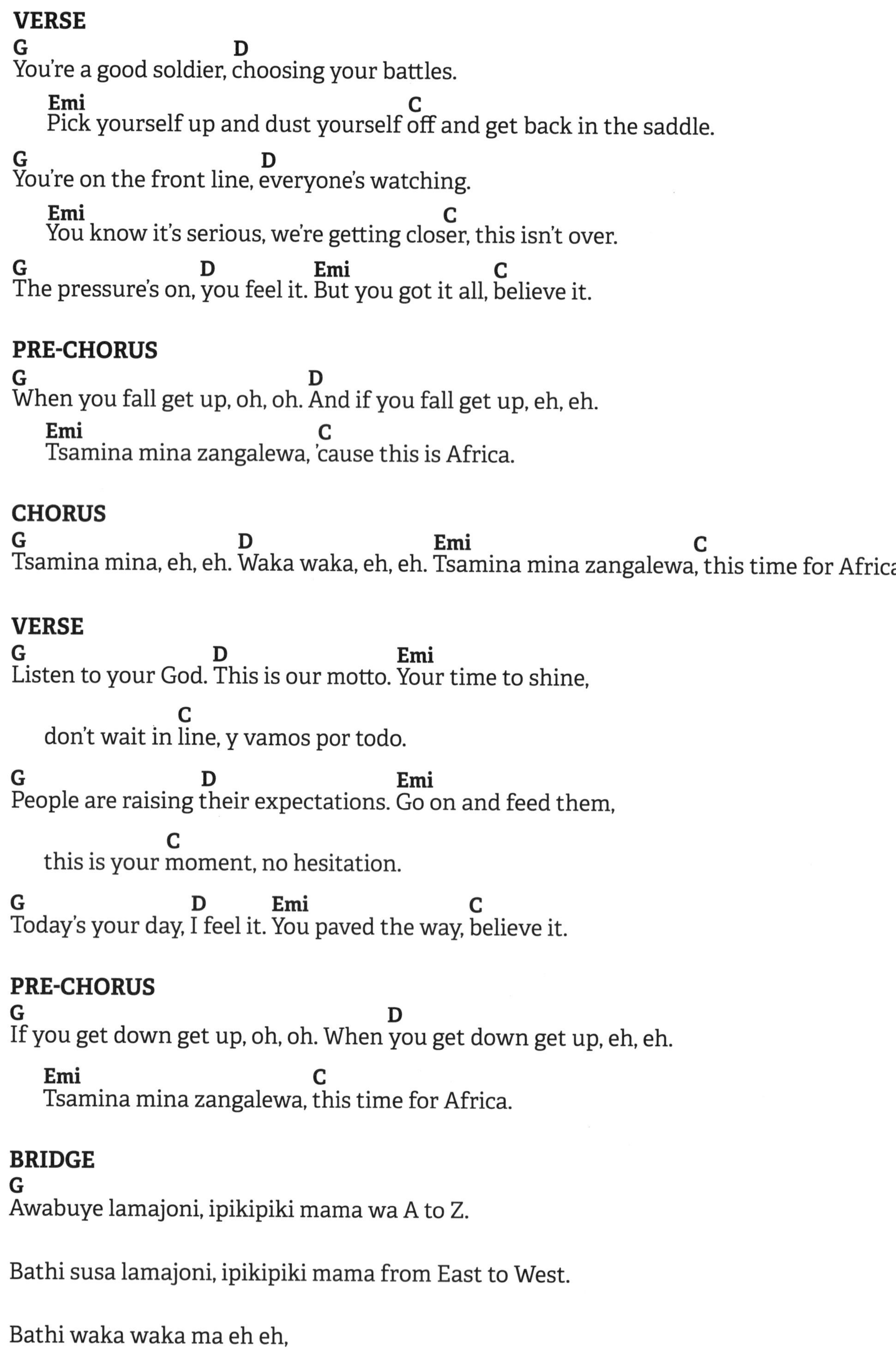

VERSE

G D
You're a good soldier, choosing your battles.

Emi C
Pick yourself up and dust yourself off and get back in the saddle.

G D
You're on the front line, everyone's watching.

Emi C
You know it's serious, we're getting closer, this isn't over.

G D Emi C
The pressure's on, you feel it. But you got it all, believe it.

PRE-CHORUS

G D
When you fall get up, oh, oh. And if you fall get up, eh, eh.

Emi C
Tsamina mina zangalewa, 'cause this is Africa.

CHORUS

G D Emi C
Tsamina mina, eh, eh. Waka waka, eh, eh. Tsamina mina zangalewa, this time for Africa.

VERSE

G D Emi
Listen to your God. This is our motto. Your time to shine,

C
don't wait in line, y vamos por todo.

G D Emi
People are raising their expectations. Go on and feed them,

C
this is your moment, no hesitation.

G D Emi C
Today's your day, I feel it. You paved the way, believe it.

PRE-CHORUS

G D
If you get down get up, oh, oh. When you get down get up, eh, eh.

Emi C
Tsamina mina zangalewa, this time for Africa.

BRIDGE

G
Awabuye lamajoni, ipikipiki mama wa A to Z.

Bathi susa lamajoni, ipikipiki mama from East to West.

Bathi waka waka ma eh eh,

Waka waka ma eh eh,

Zonk' izizwe mazibuye, 'cause this is Africa.

SECTION 9

Music Theory: A Focus on Note Length

The length of a note makes a big difference in the feel of a groove. A bass player can play the same notes and rhythms but change the feel of a song by changing whether they play short or long notes.

*Note—The next examples contain **half rests** ▬. This is a mark that tells the performer to stop playing for two beats. One half rest is the same as two quarter rests.

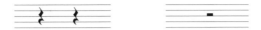

Play through this exercise, making sure to mute the note at the right time by gently touching the string with your left and/or right hand.

Here's that same exercise on a different note. To mute a note that you're fretting, simply release the pressure used to play that note in the left hand. (Don't take your finger completely off the string.)

As you listen to and learn new music, be sure to listen to the length of the notes the bass player is playing. Accurately controlling note length will make a big difference in how you fill your role and sound as a bass player.

Below is a song that has changing note lengths. The first time through the pattern, the bass plays quarter notes, each lasting one beat. The second time through, the bass plays whole notes, each lasting four beats. Then, the entire sequence repeats.

Listen carefully to the recording and match the note length.

SAIL

AWOLNATION

Take another look at these bass lines you've played before, but this time, pay careful attention to note lengths. For example, in both riffs the note played on the 5th fret is held down longer than most of the other notes. Performing these bass lines with careful attention to note length will push you forward to sounding like an accomplished bass player.

Try playing these few bass lines:

HYPNOTIZE

The Notorious BIG

MY OWN WORST ENEMY

Lit

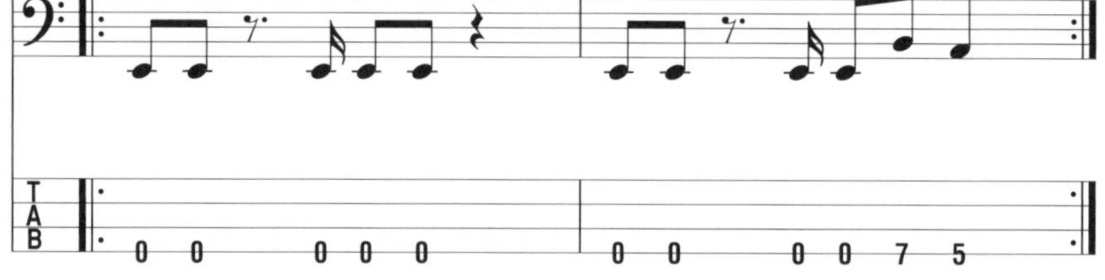

Note lengths are not always notated on the tab staff, which is one of the benefits of staff notation… and a reminder that it's important to use your ear to play these songs accurately.

Playing Bass Lines: Grooving with the Rest of the Band

Your bandmates who are learning full chords may not yet know just how important your bass playing is in making these songs sound stylistically appropriate. For this tune, keeping the notes long and smooth will match the ballad style of the tune.

HEY THERE DELILAH

Plain White T's

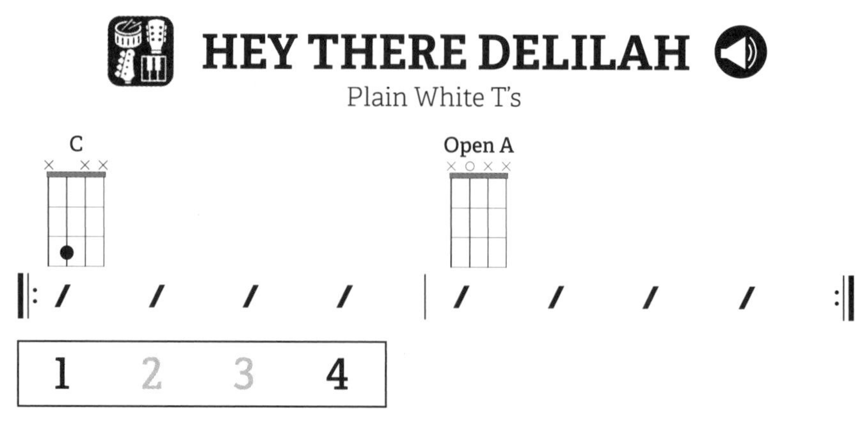

This song is much more rhythmically dynamic than the last. Keeping the notes short helps to drive that rhythm.

HAITI

Arcade Fire

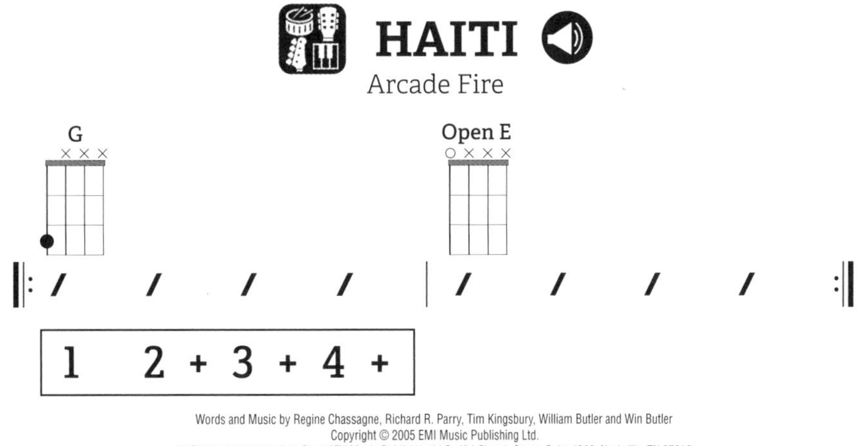

This song features a harsh attack on the drums and guitar; try to match that on the bass by plucking or picking the strings with a bit more force.

WILD THING

The Troggs

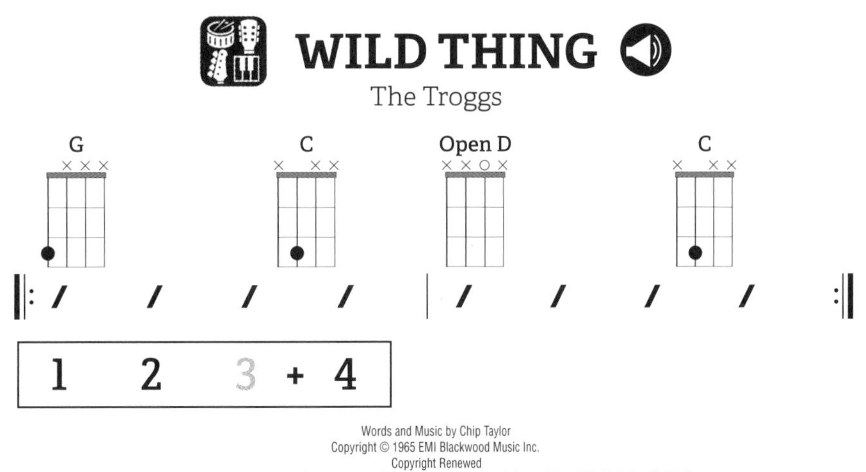

Your bandmates are focusing on the chord progression below. The way you choose to play the root notes G, D, E, and C will make a big difference in how the song sounds.

This progression can be found in many songs from the last 60 years, including "Where Is the Love?" "Bored to Death," "Demons," "Apologize," "The Edge of Glory," "Someone Like You," and hundreds of others. Try it with the Chorus of the pop song "The Edge of Glory" by Lady Gaga.

For a pop dance track, playing on every beat is typical. This reinforces the kick drum and helps drive the music.

THE EDGE OF GLORY

Lady Gaga

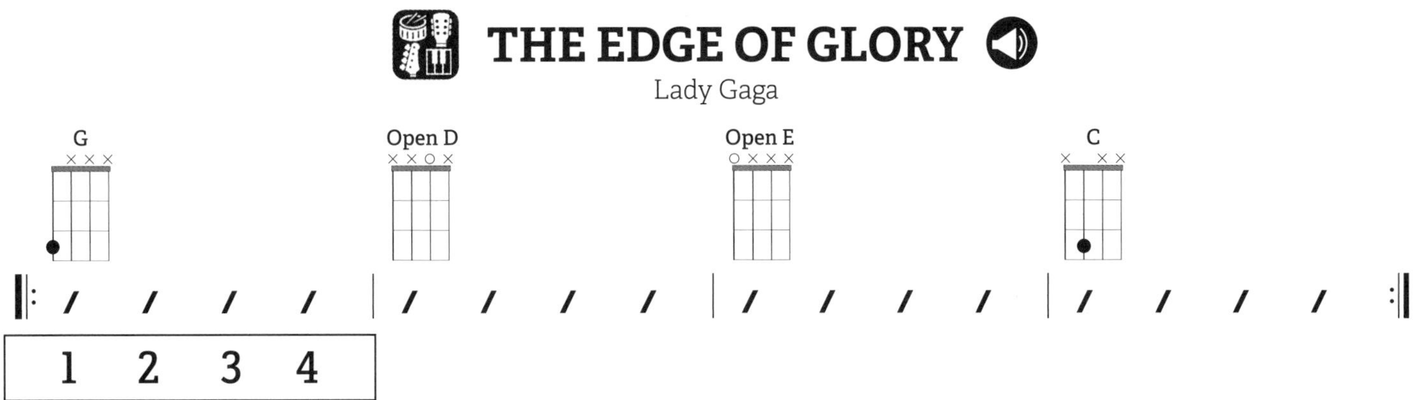

Composition: Verse and Chorus

Now that you know more notes—and your bandmates know more chords—you can use them to compose songs. Create a new four-chord verse and chorus, using any of the chords your bandmates have already learned (A, Ami, C, D, E, Emi, and G). Try using a syncopated rhythm for either your verse or chorus.

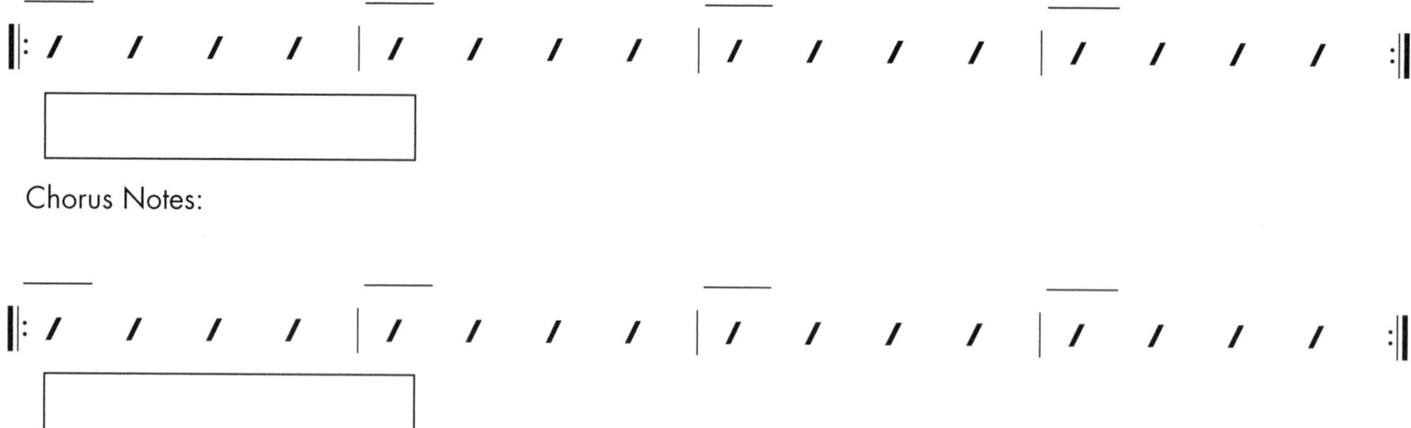

Improvisation: Major Pentatonic Scale

The **major pentatonic scale** looks a lot like the minor pentatonic scale. The only difference between the two scales is which note feels like home, or the **tonic**.

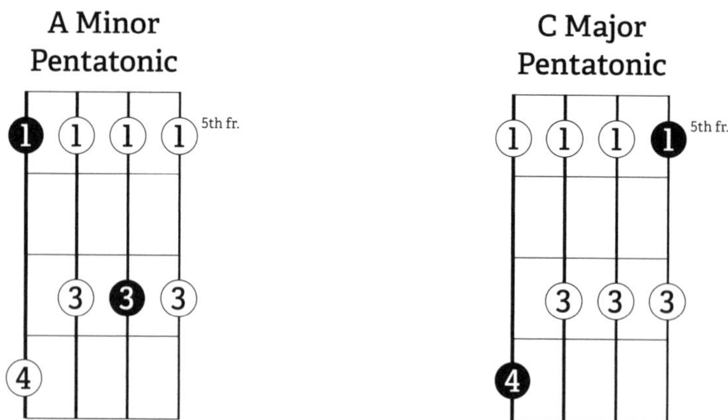

Try this out over a few familiar progressions.

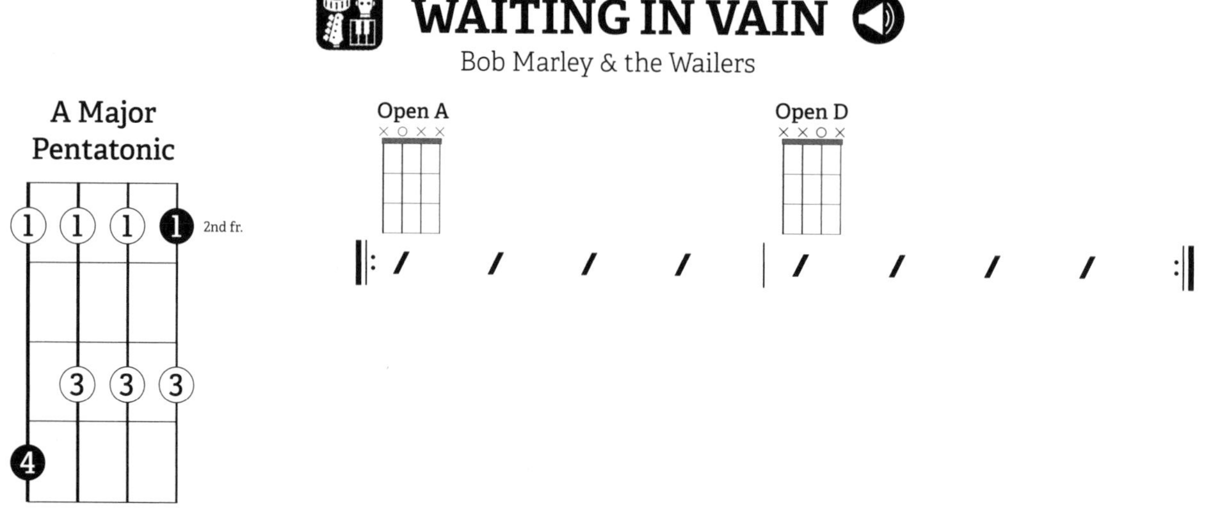

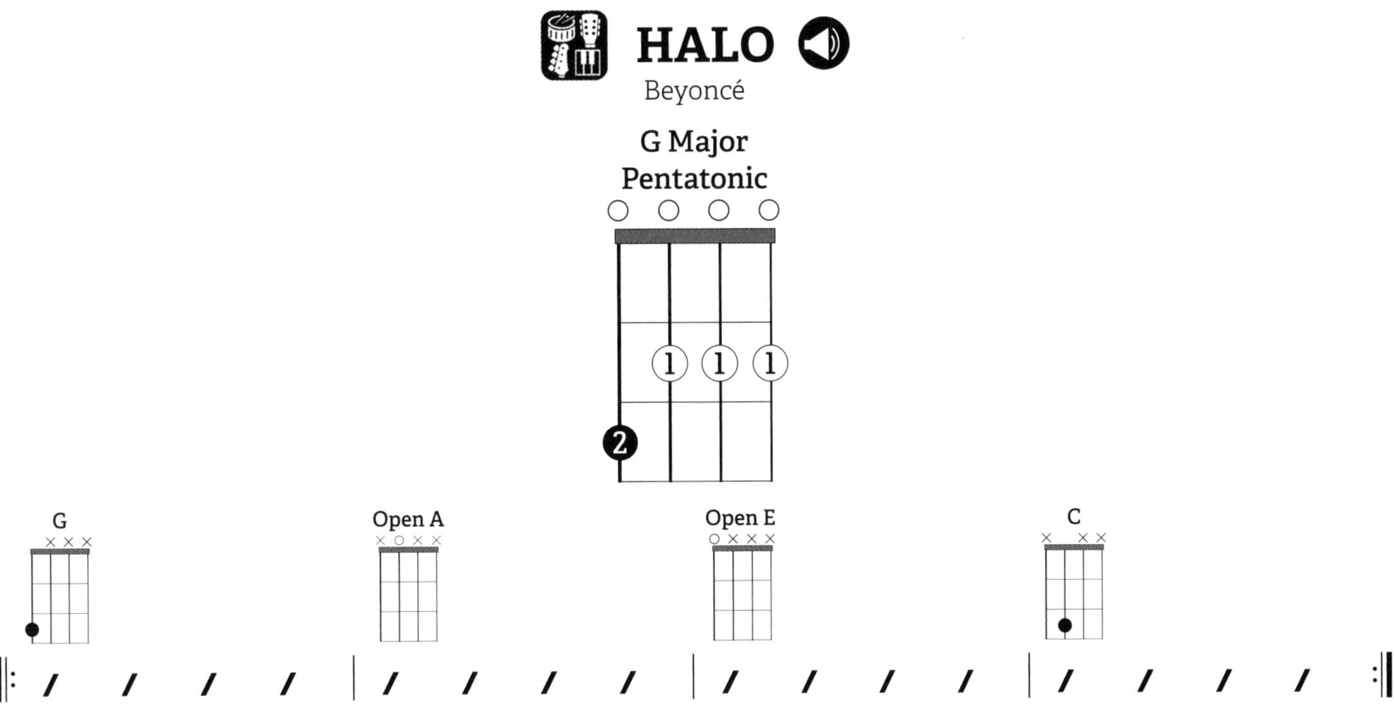

Full Band Song: BEST DAY OF MY LIFE

American Authors

Form of Recording: Intro–Verse–Pre-Chorus–Chorus–Verse–Pre-Chorus–Chorus–Bridge–Chorus

In the fourth bar of the Pre-Chorus, there is a measure with no chord. Don't play during that measure of music.

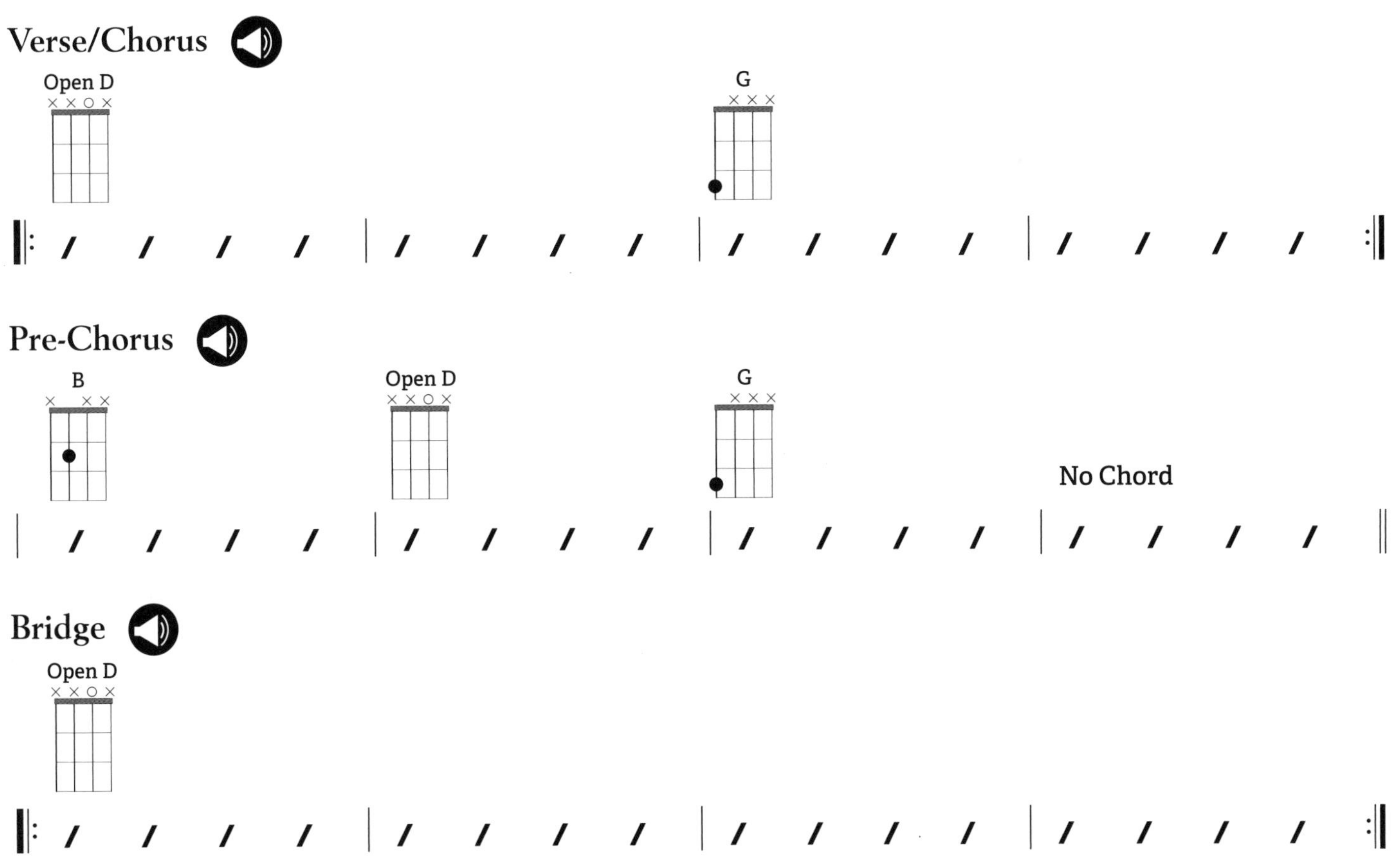

For this song, you can use the following rhythm for the Verse and Chorus:

1	2	3	4

And this one for the Pre-Chorus:

1	2	3	4

You can use notes from the following scale to improvise or come up with your own bass lines.

D Major Pentatonic

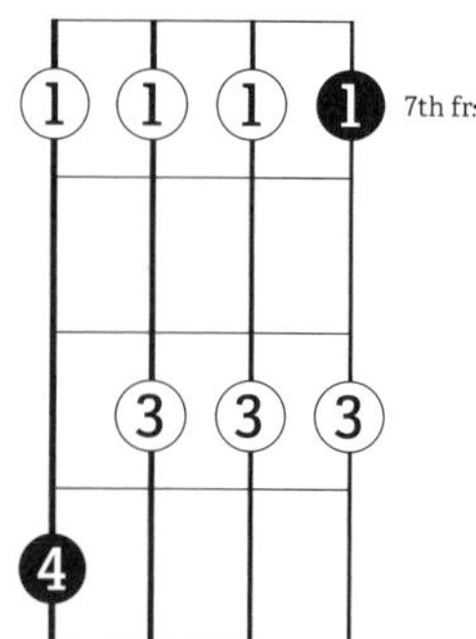

VERSE

D
I had a dream so big and loud. I jumped so high I touched the clouds.

G
Whoa-o-o-o-o-oh. Whoa-o-o-o-o-oh.

D
I stretched my hands out to the sky. We danced with monsters through the night.

G
Whoa-o-o-o-o-oh. Whoa-o-o-o-o-oh.

PRE-CHORUS

D (bass plays B) D G
I'm never gonna look back, whoa. I'm never gonna give it up, no. Please don't wake me now.

CHORUS

D G
Wo-o-o-o-oo! This is gonna be the best day of my life, my life.

D G
Wo-o-o-o-oo! This is gonna be the best day of my life, my life.

VERSE

D
I howled at the moon with friends. And then the sun came crashing in.

G
Whoa-o-o-o-o-oh. Whoa-o-o-o-o-oh.

D
But all the possibilities, no limits just epiphanies.

G
Whoa-o-o-o-o-oh. Whoa-o-o-o-o-oh.

BRIDGE

D
I hear it calling outside my window.

I feel it in my soul, soul.

The stars were burning so bright,

The sun was out 'til midnight.

I say we lose control, control.

SECTION 10

Instrument Technique: Slides

A **slide** is when you move from one note to another by sliding your finger from one fret to another; slides add another form of phrasing.

An example of a bass slide can be found in the appropriately named song, "Slide," by Slave, which starts with a slide up and down the E string. To play this, just play an open E, next apply pressure with a left-hand finger at around the 1st fret and slide your finger up to about the 12th fret, then back down the neck.

Try it in the following situations. All of these examples use the D minor pentatonic scale. 

D Minor Pentatonic

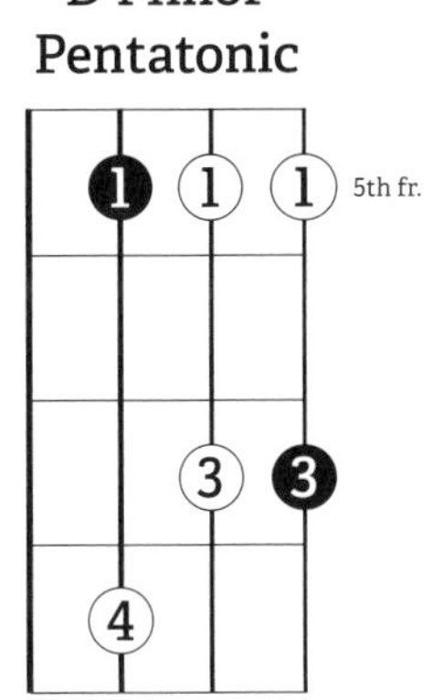

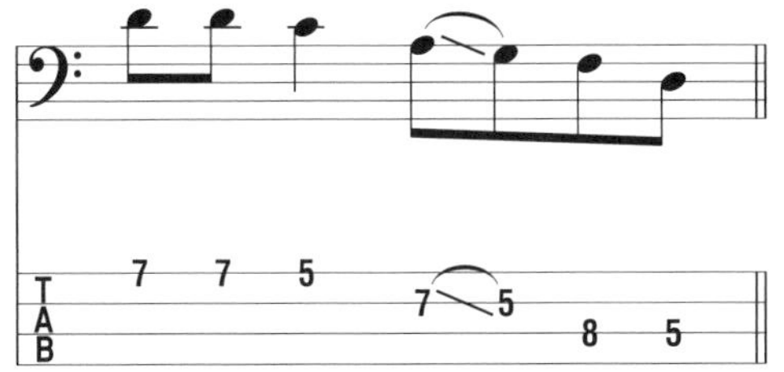

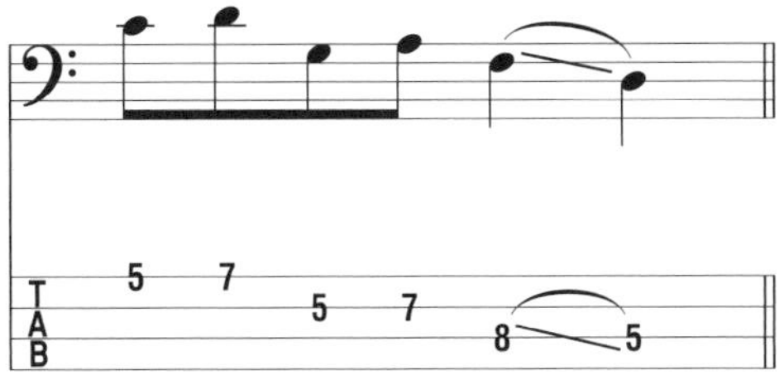

When sliding into a note like in the third example above, start one or two frets lower than the written note and slide into it.

Music Theory: Passing Tones

One application of scales is adding **passing tones** to your performance. It's common for a bassist to play only root notes of chords, but passing tones can be added to create variety. Pick a note from a scale you've learned that is in between the note you are moving from and the note you are moving to. Then, try substituting it for the note on beat 4 of a song you've previously learned.

To add a passing tone to the following song by the Isley Brothers, play the B on fret 2 of string 3 on beat "4+" of each measure.

SHOUT

The Isley Brothers

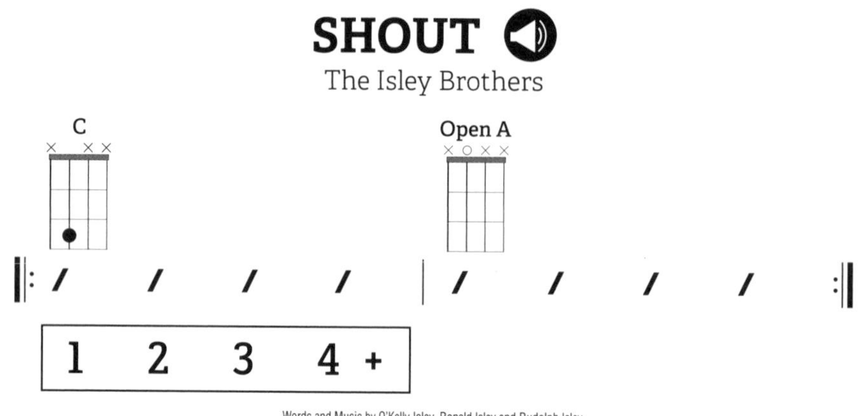

OYE COMO VA

Santana

ZOMBIE

The Cranberries

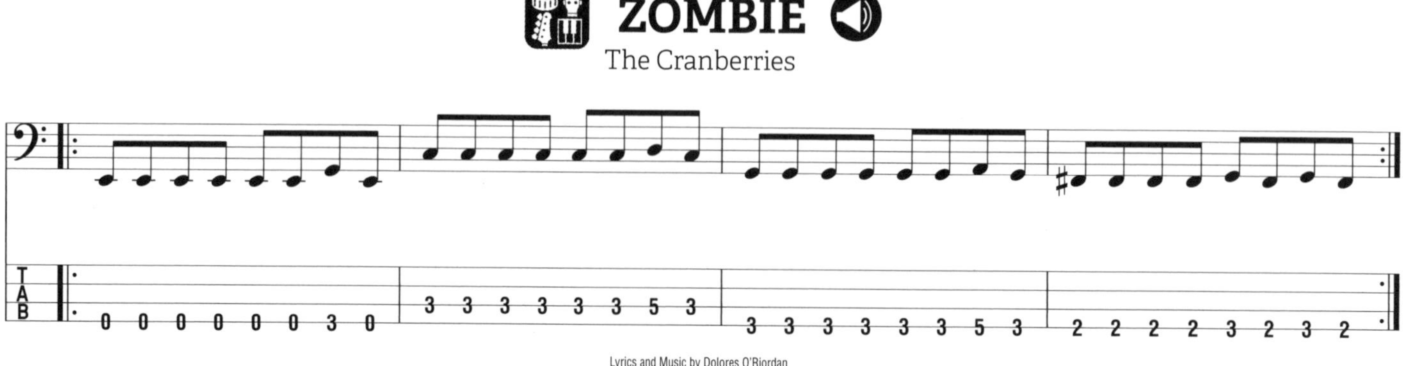

Write a chord progression below. Then, pick appropriate passing tones for the fourth beat of each measure. Remember, the pitch of the passing tone should fall in between the pitches of the root notes being played in each measure.

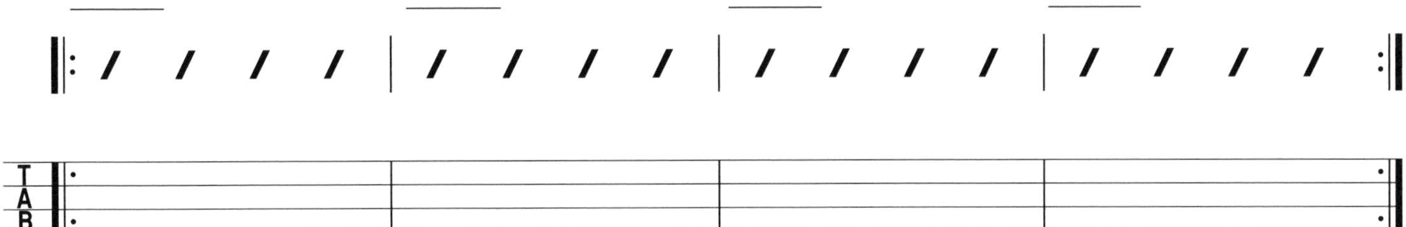

Music Theory: Applying Slides

Here are some more bass lines that contain slides.

For this riff, slide up to the 7th fret on the D string. Then, play the note on the 10th fret of the G string. Finally, play the 12th fret of the D string and slide back down to get your hand in position to play the 5th fret of the A string again.

Here's a similar bass line that also uses slides:

You may be asking, "...but what note do I slide from to play the note on the 14th fret of the D string?" The answer: it doesn't really matter. Don't worry too much about picking a starting note. Instead, aim to land on the 14th fret right in time.

Try this technique in the next song—just don't overdo it. A slide will sound cool every once in a while, but it shouldn't be the main feature of the song.

Full Band Song: KICK, PUSH

Lupe Fiasco

Form of Recording: Verse–Chorus–Verse–Chorus–Verse–Chorus

This song combines slides and passing tones. Listen carefully to the recording for the timing of both.

VERSE

First got it when he was six, didn't know any tricks. Matter fact,
First time he got on it he slipped, landed on his hip and bust his lip.
For a week he had to talk with a lisp, like this.
Now we can end the story right here,
But shorty didn't quit, it was something in the air, yea.
He said it was somethin' so appealing. He couldn't fight the feelin'.
Somethin' about it, he knew he couldn't doubt it, couldn't understand it,
Brand it, since the first kickflip he landed, uh. Labeled a misfit, abandoned,
Ca-kunk, ca-kunk, kunk. His neighbors couldn't stand it, so he was banished to the park.
Started in the morning, wouldn't stop till after dark, yea.
When they said "it's getting late in here, so I'm sorry young man, there's no skating here."

CHORUS

So we kick, push, kick, push, kick, push, kick, push, coast.
And the way he roll just a rebel to the world with no place to go.
So we kick, push, kick, push, kick, push, kick, push, coast.
So come and skate with me, just a rebel looking for a place to be.
So let's kick, and push, and coast.

VERSE

Uh, uh, uh. My man got a lil' older, became a better roller (yea).
No helmet, hell-bent on killin' himself, was what his momma said.
But he was feelin' himself, got a lil' more swagger in his style.
Met his girlfriend, she was clappin' in the crowd.
Love is what was happening to him now, uh. He said "I would marry you but I'm engaged to
These aerials and varials, and I don't think this board is strong enough to carry two."
She said "beau, I weigh 120 pounds. Now, lemme make one thing clear, I don't need to ride yours,
I got mine right here." So she took him to a spot he didn't know about,
Somewhere in the apartment parking lot, she said, "I don't normally take dates in here."
Security came and said, "I'm sorry there's no skating here."

CHORUS
So they kick, push, kick, push, kick, push, kick, push, coast.
And the way they roll, just lovers intertwined with no place to go.
And so they kick, push, kick, push, kick, push, kick, push, coast.
So come and skate with me, just a rebel looking for a place to be.
So let's kick, and push, and coast.

VERSE
Yea uh, yea, yea. Before he knew he had a crew that wasn't no punk
In they Spitfire shirts and SB Dunks. They would push, till they couldn't skate no more.
Office buildings, lobbies wasn't safe no more.
And it wasn't like they wasn't getting chased no more,
Just the freedom is better than breathing, they said.
An escape route, they used to escape out when things got crazy they needed to break out.
(They'd head) to any place with stairs, and good grinds the world was theirs, uh.
And they four wheels would take them there,
Until the cops came and said, "There's no skating here."

CHORUS
So they kick, push, kick, push, kick, push, kick, push, coast.
And the way they roll, just rebels without a cause with no place to go.
And so they kick, push, kick, push, kick, push, kick, push, coast.
So come roll with me, just a rebel looking for a place to be.
So let's kick, and push, and coast.

SECTION 11

Music Theory: Blues Scale

BAD

Michael Jackson

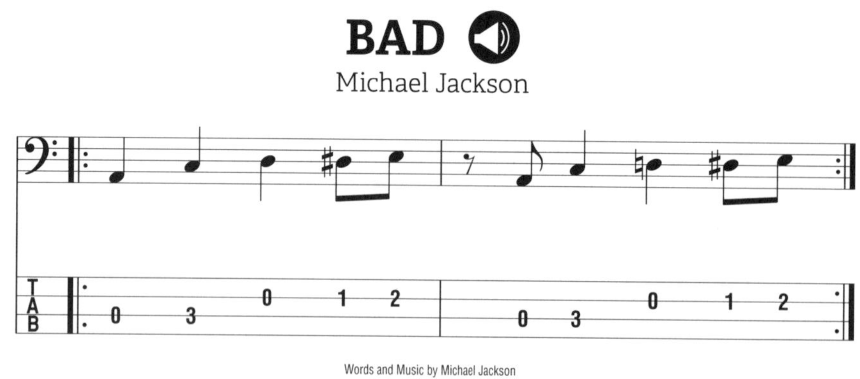

SUNSHINE OF YOUR LOVE

Cream

Both of the preceding examples use the **blues scale**. You can use this scale to write riffs or play solos. The blues scale is the minor pentatonic scale with an added "blue" note. There is no fret reference number shown on the scale grid below, because this scale shape can be moved up and down the neck of the bass, just like the pentatonic scales.

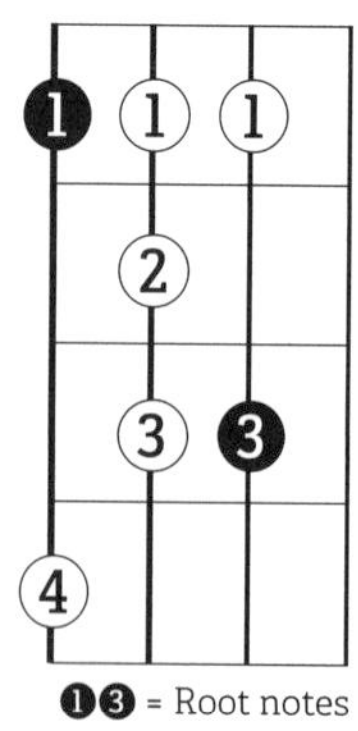

❶❸ = Root notes

Let's try the blues scale with "Evil Ways" by Santana, transposed to D minor (originally in G minor). Also try playing the blues scale over earlier Jam Tracks.

Santana

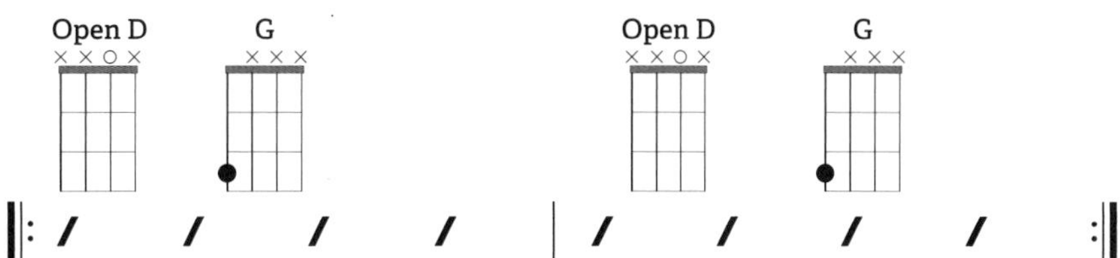

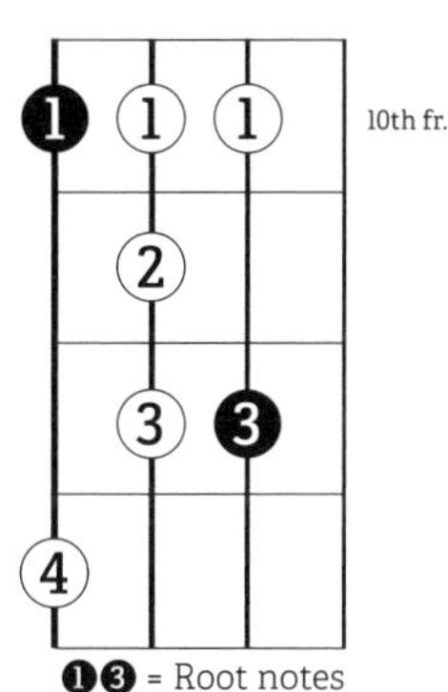

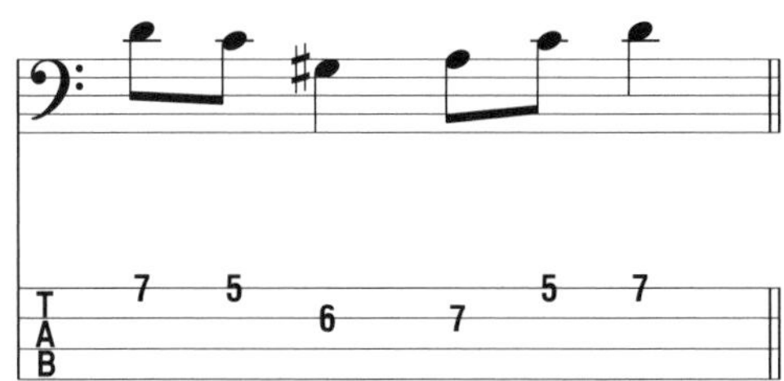

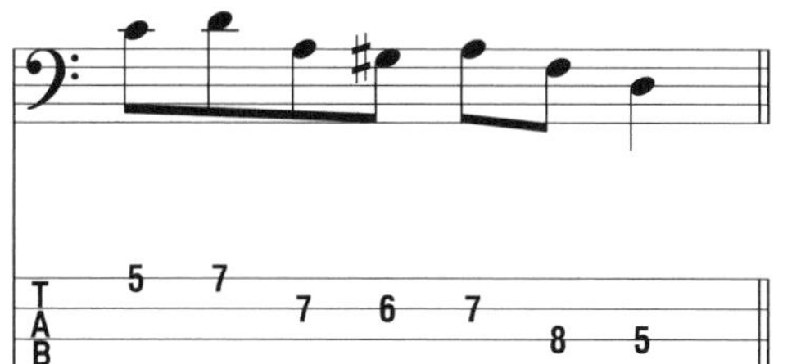

Music Theory: Chords as Riffs

While many songs have chords that last a whole bar, some songs change chords quickly. This can make the chords sound more melodic, like riffs. Many of these chords as riffs are instantly recognizable, even before someone starts singing. Bassists can play root notes of those chords along with the guitar or keyboard player to emphasize the changing chords. This is extremely popular in classic rock music. Here are a couple examples:

STRAY CAT STRUT

Stray Cats

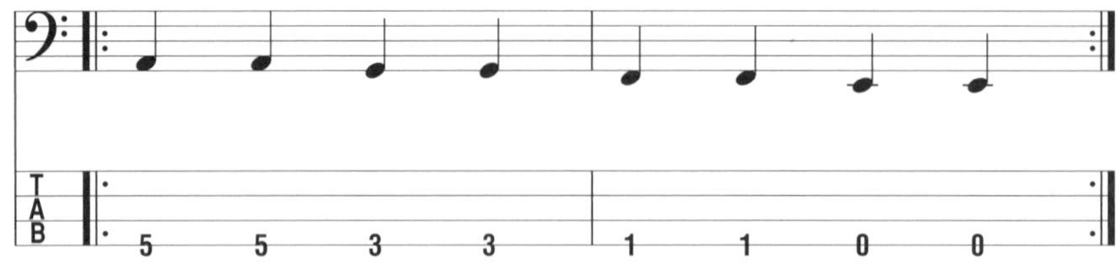

SMELLS LIKE TEEN SPIRIT

Nirvana

Composition: Composing with Power Chords 

Rock guitarists use simple two-note "chords" called **power chords**. As a bass player, you can often just play the root note of the power chord. Compare the diagrams below:

A5

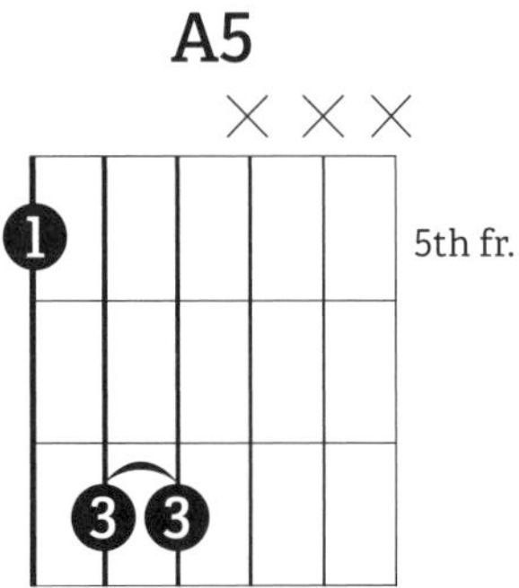

A

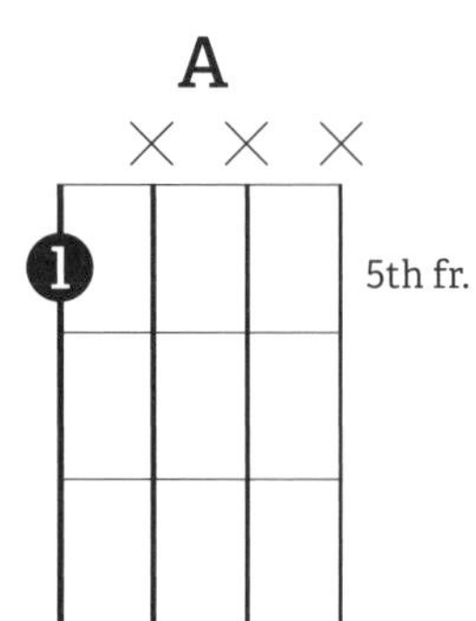

To write a song with power chords, pick a string number (3 or 4) and a fret number (1–10). Play the root of the power chord at that location with your first finger on that fret and string. Pick four power chords (notes) this way and write a rhythm to play them with.

Full Band Song: UMBRELLA

Rihanna

Form of Recording: Intro–Verse–Chorus–Verse–Chorus–Bridge–Chorus

For this song, you can play these notes in the first Verse:

Verse

In the Chorus section, you can play sustained notes:

Chorus

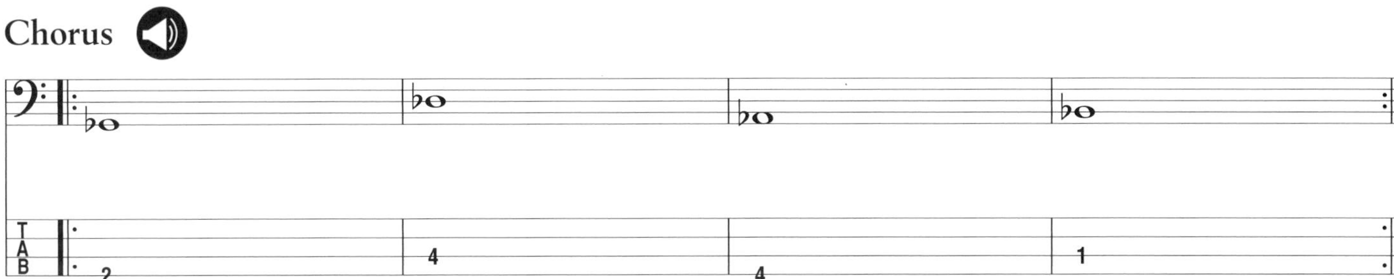

Often in music, material is repeated but with different endings. To show this, we can write **first and second endings** in the notation. These are the measures under the brackets labeled "1." and "2." To play this, perform the first four measures of Verse 2 below and then repeat. When playing it the second time, skip the first ending and play the second ending.

Verse 2

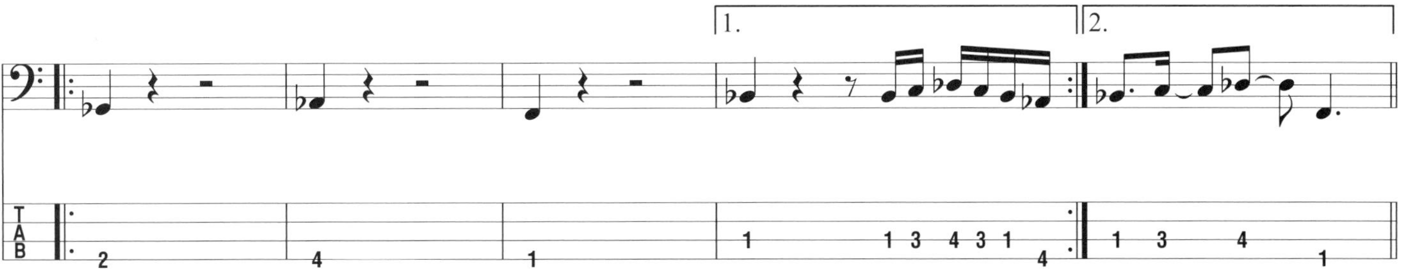

The Bridge also has a first and second ending. Play the four measures before the repeat sign the first time, then skip the first ending the second time and jump to the second ending.

Bridge

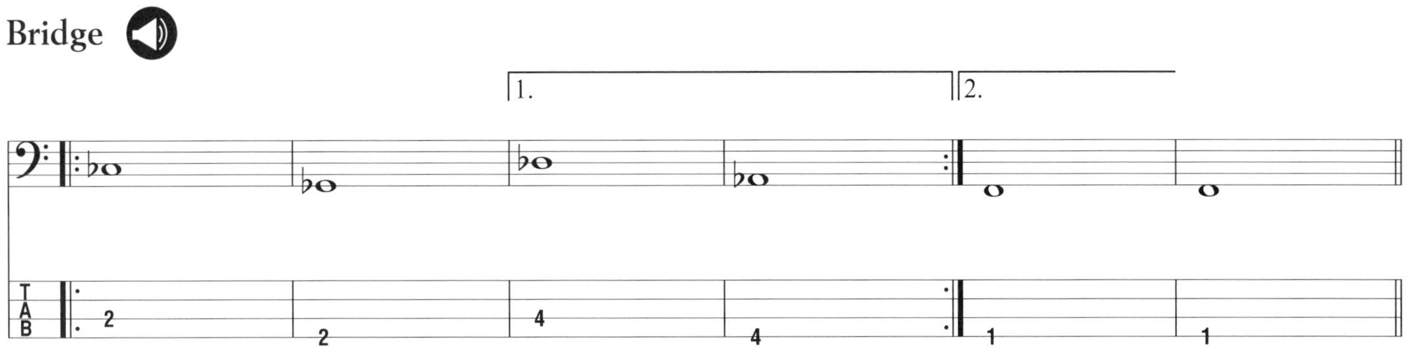

You can use the B♭ blues scale to improvise over all the sections except the Bridge.

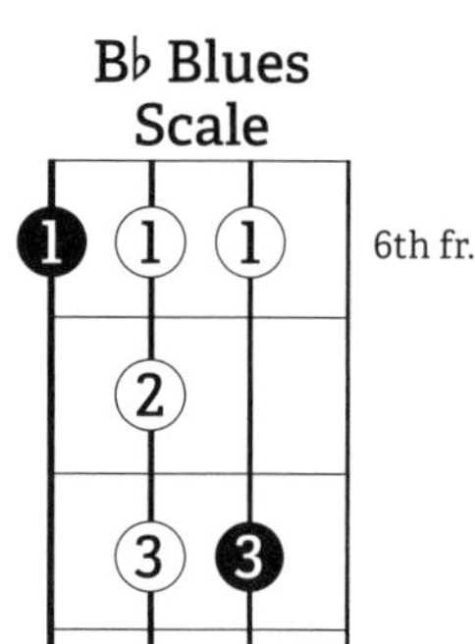

VERSE

G♭5 A♭5
You have my heart, and we'll never be worlds apart.

F5 B♭5
Maybe in magazines, but you'll still be my star.

G♭5 A♭5
Baby, 'cause in the dark you can't see shiny cars.

F5 B♭5
And that's when you need me there, with you I'll always share, because...

CHORUS

G♭5 D♭5 A♭5
When the sun shines, we'll shine together. Told you I'd be here forever.

B♭5
Said I'll always be your friend. Took an oath, I'mma stick it out 'til the end.

G♭5 D♭5 A♭5
Now that it's raining more than ever, know that we'll still have each other.

B♭5 G♭5
You can stand under my umbrella. You can stand under my umbrella.

D♭5 A♭5
(Ella, ella, eh, eh, eh.) Under my umbrella.

B♭5 G♭5
(Ella, ella, eh, eh, eh.) Under my umbrella.

D♭5 A♭5
(Ella, ella, eh, eh, eh.) Under my umbrella.

B♭5
(Ella, ella, eh, eh, eh, eh, eh, eh.)

VERSE

G♭5 A♭5
These fancy things, will never come in between.

F5 B♭5
You're part of my entity, here for infinity.

G♭5 A♭5
When the war has took its part, when the world has dealt its cards,

F5 B♭5
If the hand is hard, together we'll mend your heart.

BRIDGE

C♭5 G♭5
You can run into my arms. It's OK, don't be alarmed.

D♭5 A♭5
Come here to me. There's no distance in between our love.

C♭5 G♭5
So go on and let the rain pour.

F5
I'll be all you need and more, because...

SECTION 12

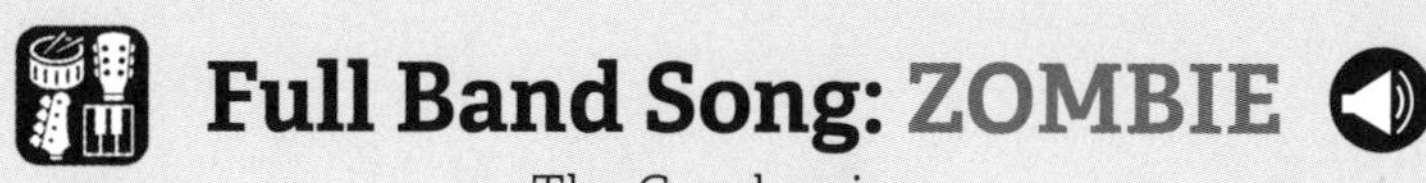

Form of Recording: Intro–Verse–Chorus–Verse–Chorus–Bridge–Chorus–Outro

This song has a Verse and Chorus that are identical. What changes between the Verse and Chorus? How might you, as the bass player, help to highlight these differences?

Here is the whole song. We've added the chord names to the top of the tab for reference. It's always good to keep in mind what chords your fellow musicians are playing.

Intro/Verse/Chorus

Bridge/Outro

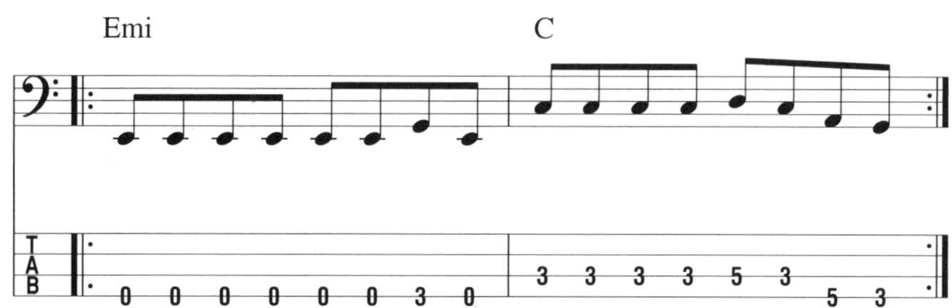

VERSE
Emi   **Cmaj7**   **G**   **D**
Another head hangs lowly, child is slowly taken.

Emi   **Cmaj7**   **G**   **D**
And the violence caused such silence. Who are we mistaken?

        Emi   **Cmaj7**   **G**   **D**
But you see it's not me, it's not my family. In your head, in your head they are fighting,

           Emi   **Cmaj7**
With their tanks, and their bombs, and their bombs, and their guns.

         G   **D**
In your head, in your head they are crying.

CHORUS
        E5   **C5**   **G5**   **D5**
In your head, in your head, zombie, zombie, zombie, hey, hey.

               E5   **C5**   **G5**   **D5**
What's in your head, in your head, zombie, zombie, zombie, hey, hey, hey?

VERSE
Emi   **Cmaj7**   **G**   **D**
Another mother's breakin' heart is taking over.

Emi   **Cmaj7**   **G**   **D**
When the violence causes silence, we must be mistaken.

        Emi   **Cmaj7**   **G**   **D**
It's the same old theme since nineteen-sixteen. In your head, in your head they're still fighting,

           Emi   **Cmaj7**
With their tanks, and their bombs, and their bombs, and their guns.

          G   **D**
In your head, in your head they are dying.

CHORUS
        E5   **C5**   **G5**   **D5**
In your head, in your head, zombie, zombie, zombie, hey, hey.

               E5   **C5**   **G5**   **D5**
What's in your head, in your head, zombie, zombie, zombie. Hey, hey, hey?